"Organizations are tricky things, and it takes someone with clever insight to decode their mysteries. Ferraro's work is as real as it is lively, diagnosing and treating the common diseases of modern business.

Put simply, Ferraro's savvy approach strikes at the core of company business dilemmas, offering solid, well-informed ...

... oi Ed.D., RN
rofessor of Business
Nazarene University

"Judy wrote an inspiring book on sales and leadership that I will use to influence those in my sphere of care."

— Jean Pitzo
CEO

"Judy's book is a must read for any executive because it touches on critical issues that are prevalent in every industry. From dissecting management types to providing concrete suggestions for improving and motivating a sluggish sales force, this book is a surefire way to stimulate, challenge and inspire executives. I especially enjoyed how Judy tackles complex subjects in a simple manner. A healthy mixture of good experience, psychology and advice makes this book a perfect combination."

— Lisa Gordon
Editor

"I always look forward to my issue of *Scrap Magazine* just to read Judy's columns. I find her advice to be inspirational, and always use it to motivate our sales force and to simulate discussion and ideas that lead to closer customer engagement. When I read her words, I hear her voice. It is like having a conversation with that confidant or mentor that you love to talk to."

— Albert Cozzi
Scrap Industry Executive

"Judy's observations are painfully honest. Her mix of analysis, helpful advice and humor makes her the boss we all wish we had."

— Barbara Pinto
WYCC PBS Chicago

"Ms. Ferraro has written an insightful collection of advice, ranging from the cliché to the intensely experiential, which is a most valuable refresher for middle managers and core reference for readers new to the management ranks."

— Jim Gordon
Consultant

ON SALES, LEADERSHIP & OTHER HELPFUL BUSINESS STUFF

A collection of columns offering sales
and leadership insight and advice from
award-winning columnist

JUDY FERRARO

FORWARD & DEDICATION

I can remember writing poetry and stories from the moment I learned how to put a pen to paper. I shared most of my writings with my mother, who loved them all. She thoughtfully saved them in drawers and boxes along with the cards, leaves ironed in wax paper, and spray-painted macaroni on cardboard artworks. She encouraged me to write and I did.

My penchant for writing solidified when my 5th grade teacher, Mrs. Hooper, named me editor of the Room 18 Gazette. I was assigned to write a column for the newsletter and edit those of other contributors. There was nothing more important to me than the Gazette and delivering quarterly mimeographed masterpieces to my classmates and Mrs. Hooper, who believed in me. I had been empowered before I understood the word. That's what great parents, teachers, coaches and business leaders do.

Fast-forward nearly 40 years later. While I never stopped writing, most of what I wrote was collected in boxes and placed on a shelf. I sold my scrap metal company in 1998 and the president of that company, Frank Cozzi, was looking for participation in the company newsletter. He immediately embraced my interest in writing and piled on assignments. I remember being pretty stoked about being noticed for my talent and feeling empowered to use my creativity, much like my experience with Mrs. Hooper. I wrote articles about customers and other topics of interest. I was having so much fun that I was inspired to write a children's book called *Once Upon a Popcan* about a guy named Al Luminum who could live many lives and go on exciting journeys through recycling.

After I started my consulting business, I was asked to present a workshop a an industry conference. Following my presentation, I was approached by the editor of the association's magazine. We had never met, but I had seen him sitting in the front row and smiling. I liked Kent Kiser before his introduction and still appreciate that contagious smile. He asked if I would be interested in writing a business column focusing on sales for *Scrap*, an industry magazine. It was like a dream come true. My column continues to run over a decade later. Kent submitted my columns to the American Society of Business Publication Editors (ASBPE). I was astonished when I walked away with a Gold Award. A life highlight! Who can say they are responsible for someone's life highlight? Thank you, Kent Kiser.

This leads me to why I wrote this book. Time after time, my readers and Kent have suggested I compile my columns into a book to make them more accessible. That possibility had never occurred to me. This time it was my readers and publisher who unknowingly unleashed my creativity.

I am blessed to be in the presence of people who believe in me and glad I had the wisdom to run with their ideas. I admire and dedicate this book to:

- Eleanor Ferraro, my mother, who encouraged me to read, write, dance, sing, draw and be funny.

- Mrs. Hooper, my 5th grade teacher, who assigned me a task that later became my passion.

- Frank Cozzi, who, without seeing anything I wrote, saw my enthusiasm and went with it.

- Kent Kiser, who changed my life by asking me to write a column for his magazine, another marcher in the parade of people who hadn't any idea if I could actually write. I'm also grateful to him for submitting my columns, unbeknownst to me, that resulted in an award. When Kent called to tell me I had won, I sat at my desk weeping because I had realized a dream. I would have never submitted the columns myself or thought an award was possible.

- And, lastly, all those who have faithfully read my columns over the years and suggested I put them into book form. You have all influenced my life and empowered and encouraged me to do what I like best.

Thank you for that.

ALSO BY JUDY FERRARO:

If I Catch You, I Will Kill You

A Childhood Sexual Abuse Survivor
Redefines Life On Her Own Terms

Available at Amazon.com

ON SALES, LEADERSHIP & OTHER HELPFUL BUSINESS STUFF

A collection of columns offering sales
and leadership insight and advice from
award-winning columnist

JUDY FERRARO

CONTENTS

CHAPTER 1 | FINDING THE RELATIONSHIP

Asking the right questions to shorten the sales cycle

Every sale begins with a relationship. Therefore, I'd like to begin your reading of this book the same way—with a relationship. I begin by sharing a story about the building and solidification of a relationship.

I've been involved with the recycling industry for many years, first as a salesperson for a few scrap metal companies (including my own) and now as an industry consultant. While I consult in a variety of industries, the scrap industry is like the mafia, hard to leave. People in the recycling industry say things like "I've been in for 12" or "I've been in for 30," as if serving some sort of sentence. I've been in for three decades with no real desire to ever leave.

Just before 9/11, I founded Judy Ferraro & Associates Inc. to help develop other sales professionals and share the skills that brought me success during more than 30 years as a sales professional. Though my company has worked in many industries and markets, recycling kept calling me back. Making a sales call in the scrap industry is as natural to me as a fade away jump shot was to Michael Jordan. I'm certainly not comparing myself to "Air" Jordan, but I know how to develop the daily consistency and perseverance necessary to make the right number of calls and what to say on those calls—what it takes to develop and maintain business.

Based on my experience, developing relationships with both customers and prospects is what makes or breaks a sale. If a prospect or customer realizes their salesperson is motivated by a personal agenda, the sale will go sour. We'd all like to think "people like to do business with people they like." But contemporary buyers are savvy and deliberate in their approach. They are rewarded for protecting revenues and generating savings for their companies and trained to resist the relationship. So how does a salesperson overcome resistance and build a successful relationship?

First, I'll tell you what not to do. Years ago, I remember being thrilled to schedule an appointment at one of Chicago's premier industrial scrap accounts. When I arrived, Mr. Prospect brought me into a conference room that was so antiseptic I could have performed surgery there. He began the visit saying, "I'm not going to change vendors." Not an encouraging start to the process for me.

I launched into telling Mr. Prospect about my company and all the fabulous things I could do for him. I tried convincing him his life would be better if he'd just give my firm a shot. Basically, I did what I now call the "info dump." I learned little about Mr. Prospect and his company. I went in with my own agenda. I'm sure my motives were as transparent as glass to this smart businessman. What he heard was "Blah, blah, blah! All about me." Not an impressive first impression.

Though I got the account a few years later, I could've shortened the sales cycle by asking the right questions sooner in the relationship. Probing with open-ended questions would have encouraged Mr. Prospect to talk about himself and his company. It would've been a better way to open the lines of communication. When you get the right information, you can more easily match your company's services to the prospect's specific needs. Seems obvious now, but at the time I just didn't know how to do that. All I knew then was how to drone on about the great stuff my company could do.

Without the right information, a salesperson can't even create an effective proposal. Everything is generic—the sales call, the proposal, the presentation. The sales cycle is lengthened because you're still gathering information at the third meeting that should've been gathered during the first. I encourage salespeople to bring an agenda to all sales calls to ensure they know what information is needed to move the sale to the next step.

While conducting interviews with a sales team preparing for my training program, I spoke with a quiet man who appeared extremely organized and motivated. I asked him questions about his career in the trucking industry and how he came to the scrap business. He began describing his goals. He seemed incredibly focused, so I asked if he was always so driven. By asking the right questions, I found out he attributed much of his focus to being an only child. Later, I shared with him that my husband and I were raising an only child. I asked him about the relationship with his parents and the special challenges of being an only child. Our conversation opened up and we began to learn a lot about one another.

He told me his greatest challenge in his personal life stemmed from marrying a woman from a large family. The family gatherings—especially Christmas—were overwhelming to him as an only child. He and his wife now have two children of their own. With the addition of even more children, the family get-togethers are as loud and joyous as ever. "There are kids and presents everywhere," he told me. "Every year someone even dresses up like Santa Claus and hands out gifts."

I asked him how long it took to adjust to the new and extremely festive environment. He said he was welcomed with open arms from the start, "and before I knew it, I was Santa Claus." It doesn't get much better than that.

I liked his warm and wonderful story and wrote it down immediately. I told him that I hoped my only child would have as nice an anecdote to tell someday. Before we knew it, we had a relationship.

Chapter Takeaway:

CHAPTER 2 | SALES AS A CAREER

Identifying what it takes for personal and team success

When I was a child, my vision of a typical salesman was based on television: Ward Cleaver of "Leave It to Beaver" fame. Each evening, Ward returned home, briefcase in hand, and recounted the trials and tribulations of his sales workday while wife June listened cheerfully in her apron and pearls and served the family a wholesome dinner.

It didn't dawn on me until much later that Ward, like many of us sales professionals, probably wondered how he ended up as a salesman. Not that there's anything wrong with sales. It's just not one of those careers that kids aspire to like being an athlete, firefighter or teacher.

Possibly because you are an extrovert, you had a friend, relative or teacher remark, "What a great salesperson you'd make!" Even then, the assumption was that you'd be selling some kind of mainstream product or service, such as cars or insurance. Certainly not something as esoteric as scrap!

Many of the salespeople in family businesses—recycling or otherwise—get the sales job because they're the talkative ones. While being a good conversationalist can be helpful, it isn't the core ingredient of sales success. I learned that lesson years ago while seeking to hire salespeople for my own company.

I decided to recruit fellow improvisers from my Chicago Second City comedy team to make cold calls for my company. Most of them didn't have a shy bone in their body. They were extreme extroverts on stage and could talk and talk and talk! In fact, most of them are now successful performers in Hollywood or New York. But while they were very talented at mimicking the voice of Bill Clinton, they weren't always comfortable making sales prospecting calls.

So what qualities make a good salesperson? For starters, people who take an organized approach to work and life will always have an advantage over less organized folks. Possessing the abilities to listen actively and question are essential. And further, salespeople must be able to handle rejection on a daily basis—at least at the beginning—without getting discouraged, derailed or bitter. A talented salesperson will improve over time, reducing the number of rejections and increasing closing ratios.

A friend once told me there are guests and hosts in life—you're one or the other. Salespeople are always hosts. They know how to take care of their friends, relatives and customers. They're comfortable in that position. They typically light up a room when entering, not by being gregarious and obnoxious, but by being gracious, observant and courteous at all times. The successful salesperson also dresses appropriately in a style that ideally appeals to men and women. It doesn't matter whether it is formal or casual; "appropriate" is the key word.

Importantly, a real salesperson is willing and able to make the business development calls necessary to generate business. Working with various sales teams, I meet many individuals who are dead set against cold calling or prospecting. I agree salespeople can succeed through networking, referrals or leads their company provides. Still, the ability to make an effective first (cold) call to someone who does not know you is an essential skill. Think about it. If you interviewed a sales candidate who said he or she refused to make prospecting calls, what would you do? You'd end that interview and move on to a willing candidate.

Hiring people with solid sales skills, or solid potential, should not be the end of the story, but often is. That's because few companies invest in sales training. Companies don't believe there's any special technique or skill in making a sale. Some leaders tell me their salesperson just "lucked out" and brought in a large piece of business. But is relying on luck the best way to ensure your company's success? Not so much. If you feel your salespeople are "lucking out," maybe you have the wrong team in place. Eventually, luck runs out. And when the luck runs out, so do they.

For a sales team to be successful, the sales leader must believe in the team and the team must have confidence in their leader. Properly prepared salespeople learn how to shorten their sales cycles, build and maintain solid relationships, ask for referrals, and maintain a constant flow of new business. They keep the pipeline full.

If you're building a sales team, it's important to create a synergy among your sales staff. They must be willing to share what they do know and learn what they don't know. If you are on the sales team, you are attending sales seminars, reading books on various types of selling, and networking in your industry. Don't wait for something to come your way—go and find it.

If you are a tenured sales professional and think you don't need sales training, think again. Does a champion sports team need to practice? Does a professional actor need to rehearse? Every professional can improve his or her skills. I attend seminars every other month and read at least six books a year pertaining to sales. Those activities are part of my annual professional development goals. What steps are you taking to enhance your own skills? If you can't rattle them off, Chapters 11 and 28 will guide you through the process.

Chapter Takeaway:

_____

_____

_____

CHAPTER 3 | BEFORE-AND-AFTER SALES TIPS

Be prepared: the "wing it" approach no longer works

In today's business world, a sale requires a great deal of research, preparation during the sales process, and a sharp proposal or presentation. Those elements can help you make the sale, while infinite follow-up afterward can help you keep the customer. Let's look at each of these sales elements in turn, starting with research.

Sales research reviews and enhances what you already know about prospects or current customers. With today's technology, there's no excuse for entering any business meeting "cold" (that is, uninformed). You can easily find out about the company's history, recent news on the firm, corporate press releases, product information, and other company details, such as its various locations, mission and news.

Simply put, research enables you to know more rather than less about your prospects and customers—and that's always a good thing. I review my customers' and prospects' websites and social media before a visit or training session to learn about any recent events or changes we might discuss. I include what I've learned in my notes or sales agenda.

"An agenda?" you reply incredulously. "Whoever heard of an agenda for a sales call?" Salespeople who are on the ball, that's who. Truth be told, an agenda is just one sales preparation technique you can use. An agenda ensures you cover all the important points during your call. After all, how many of us have walked out of a meeting, only to remember a pertinent question we should have asked?

Please note, your agenda doesn't have to be shared with your prospect or customer. It's simply a tool to guide you through the meeting, ensuring you've acquired all the information you need to prepare an accurate, thorough proposal. You can go over your notes, state the action items at the end of your meeting, and ask if the client would like to add anything before you submit a proposal.

Speaking of proposals, I'm appalled by some of the documents that salespeople— and even sales leaders—send to prospects and customers. Some proposals are too wordy, others include quotes or personal feelings from the sales rep, and many are written in conversational rather than professional language. Some proposals even look like fill-in-the-blank exercises. The biggest problem is most people writing proposals don't realize their writing skills are poor. And seldom are proposals reviewed by a colleague before being submitted. So the document is sent and the prospect/customer forms an impression of how much effort and care was devoted to crafting it.

Every proposal reflects the professional image of your company, so every one must present your firm in the best light. Salespeople rarely have a chance to present more than one proposal, so the first effort must be solid. To make sure your proposals hit the mark and everyone has the same expectations, you can provide samples of business letters and presentations for your salespeople to follow. Research is again the answer. There are thousands of shared presentations on line. If necessary, you can hire a business professional or consultant to create some standard letters and other documents to serve as templates for your team. Remember, you always want to put your company's best face forward.

Chapter Takeaway:

CHAPTER 4 | LISTEN UP!

Honing a skill to change your life both personally and professionally

On my way to an industry convention, I reviewed the two talks I was scheduled to give at the event and began wondering about the attendees. One of the talks—"Essential Tools for a Successful Sales Program"—would appeal to companies wanting to build their sales departments and individuals seeking to update their sales skills.

I wondered, though, what kind of audience the other presentation would attract. It was titled "Listen, You Might Learn Something." Let's be honest, it's risky leading a workshop that suggests the attendees may not listen well. Also, those choosing to attend the session would essentially be admitting they have questionable listening skills.

The more I thought about it, the more I worried: Will anyone show up? I confess I know a thing or two about poor listening skills. Years ago during a conversation with a close friend, she told me my listening skills were less than great. My knee-jerk reaction was to be insulted by her comment. What did she know? How could she accuse me of not being a good listener? I was a successful salesperson and business owner and you can't succeed in sales or business if you aren't a great listener, right? Her statement bothered me for weeks and eventually drove me to the dreaded self-help section of the bookstore where I furtively perused titles I thought would show me how to super sharpen my already sharp listening skills. In truth, I was concerned about my image. I didn't want anyone to discover me looking at books that might expose me as "unskilled," so I figured a disguise of some sort was in order.

I believe admitting you have a problem is the first step to solving it. I wasn't convinced I had a problem, of course, but I was open to finding out. At that time, I was also in the treacherous dating phase of my life and thought better listening skills could help me achieve a successful relationship. I certainly didn't need better listening skills to improve my sales career since I'd already achieved professional success.

I chose three books, put on dark glasses and a babushka, and stood in line to buy them. I paid cash to avoid the paper trail. After reading the first chapter of the first book, I quickly learned that I was indeed a poor listener. I listened, but not enough. The books helped me realize I was not properly sharing in my conversations, but taking them over. I was always the "funny one." My role was to fill the silence. I was sure that everyone wanted to hear what I had to say. (Notice how many times the pronoun "I" appears in this paragraph?) My habit and role were to take charge of conversations, fill the gaps, and think about my next thought even as someone else was expressing theirs.

I discovered that being a good listener is a necessary life skill and one that takes a great deal of practice. It isn't easy. It doesn't always come naturally.

Even in our personal lives, I bet there are many nights when our heads hit the pillows and we don't always know what really happened with our families during the day. We're comfortable with the "life-as-usual" approach to communication because it's familiar and just easier.

Chapter Takeaway:

CHAPTER 5 | HOW TO HIRE SALESPEOPLE

Developing a strong team through questioning and planning

Being a consultant requires me to answer countless questions about hiring and leading sales teams. Questions such as: How do I hire a salesperson? What qualities should I look for? How do I lead the person? How do I motivate him or her?

From my experience working with family-owned businesses, I've found the outgoing and personable son, daughter, niece, nephew, or grandma is the first to be appointed salesperson. Smaller, less sophisticated companies like to hire from the "inner sanctum" for various reasons—including paranoia. They want to hire a person they can trust with their "top secret" information, so they hire someone they know well or someone referred to them by a close friend. That approach may work out fine in some cases (in fact, I landed my first sales job through a friend's referral). If it does, great. If not, get ready for a struggle between your expectations and the person's inability to do the sales job.

Unfortunately, that person's poor performance can be a serious drag on your company's success. Also, it's not uncommon for such "privileged" people to be paid an unrealistic salary. Ultimately, they can become untouchables—people or teams who are difficult or impossible to fire. Sure, good leaders can usually find other ways to use their talents, but the point is this: being family or a close friend or having a fun and talkative personality doesn't automatically qualify that person to sell products or services for your company. The stakes are too high.

If you've never been in sales or don't know your limitations in that area, it's hard to know what to look for when hiring a salesperson. Remember, salespeople are trained to close the deal; when salespeople are being interviewed, that sales job is the deal. So beware. Some sales candidates are great at answering interview questions but can be less impressive once hired.

To find the best sales prospects, ask open-ended questions and allow the candidates to talk. Your job is to listen (didn't we talk about this?). Here are some questions to consider:

• What do you think of our website (which they should have reviewed before the interview)?
• What do you like most about being in sales? What do you dislike?

- What sales-related books or seminars have you read/attended in the past year? (It's important to hire a person who is willing to expand his or her sales knowledge by reading or attending seminars and workshops. This keeps them up to date with the business world and new sales methods.)
- How would you go about obtaining new business?
- How important is relationship-building in your sales efforts? Tell me some of the ways you approach that.
- Are you active in professional organizations? Which ones and why?
- What programs do you use to manage contacts? How did you choose? (Efficient salespeople use any one of several software programs to manage business contacts. Microsoft Outlook is a common choice for Windows users.)

In interviews with sales candidates, I've found it helpful to gauge their tenacity. You can do that by asking: How many times do you call on a prospect for new business? Believe it or not, 92 percent of salespeople call a prospect only four times before giving up. That leaves only 8 percent who have the tenacity to persevere. You want to hire someone in that 8-percent category.

After hiring, it is important to orient them to your company and their position in the firm. It's a good idea to have a job description, an employment contract and a formal training program that clearly outlines the expectations from your sales team. Those expectations should include your firm's compensation package and clearly define their earning potential to avoid any misunderstandings.

Remember that adrenaline, along with the fear of failure or the desire to please, will drive performance for the first 90 days—the so-called sales honeymoon. After that, reality sinks in. Leadership has expectations that must be met. The job can be more difficult than expected. Some may start to complain about the company or misbehave. By misbehave I mean blame. They'll find all sorts of excuses for their shortcomings. They'll complain: "I don't have enough time." "No one calls me back." "I have too much paperwork." "The company website is insufficient." "My territory is too large." Red flag! Red flag! Red flag!

In my experience, salespeople who offer excuses for their low productivity are rarely successful. They have a problem with rejection and accountability and may even stir up trouble within their department.

Leading a sales team isn't an easy task, especially if you don't understand salespeople. They must have goals that are challenging yet attainable. They must have excellent time management skills. Your task as a leader is to find the key motivation or "hot button" for each salesperson. For many, money is not the principal driver. For me, it was to collect a better paycheck than Shirley, my ex-boyfriend's successful sister. That's a good story—and it's found in Chapter 7.

Being a good leader of your sales team means being an attentive listener, providing assistance when needed, and following through on your actions. Resist the temptation to micromanage by making demands such as "Give me an accounting of everything you did last week." Effective sales leaders have a shared vision and know what it takes to get there. In other words, they have a plan—which is a great idea discussed in Chapter 48.

Chapter Takeaway:

_____

_____

_____

CHAPTER 6 | LEADERS BEHAVING BADLY

The number one reason most people leave their jobs

In my 20-plus years in business, I have worked with the good, the bad and the downright ugly when it comes to those in leadership positions. With the good, I've seen leaders motivate teams through praise, I've seen leaders offering incentives for results, I've seen some motivating with infectiously positive attitudes, and others empowering their teams to innovate their own direction. With the bad and ugly, I've seen leaders sabotage their teams with sarcasm, I've watched pessimistic personalities focus on what's missing, and I've witnessed others who "beat 'em up and send 'em out." And I learned from them all.

I once said to someone at a large corporation, "You have several people here earning huge salaries who could not act the way they do anywhere else and still keep their jobs." He nodded in agreement. That kind of leadership culture can get out of control. It's like dealing with children: Once you allow bad behavior, it's difficult to change.

There are countless bad behavior leadership styles that cause valued employees to leave. Below are the "Egregious Eight" in alphabetical order:

THE BLAMERS—leaders with low self-esteem and low confidence. These folks are experts in making excuses and dodging responsibility. They always have an explanation and won't take a bullet for anyone. As a result, they receive little respect from the company. Unfortunately, there's usually another dysfunctional person in upper leadership who listens to their complaints and gossip. This earns the Blamers the recognition they desire and gives the dysfunctional leader fuel for his or her next knee-jerk memo or reaction.

THE CONSENSUS BUILDERS—also known as "those who can't make a decision to save their lives." Please note that leadership by consensus drives a team crazy (not to be confused with those responsible leaders who look to their team for input). The Consensus Builders generally lack confidence in their ability and are driven by the need for approval and fear of making a bad decision. They don't realize that leading by consensus seldom achieves unity. Often the contrary is true. After all, each team member has a different perspective on everything, making it difficult to ever reach consensus.

Not surprisingly, teams of consensus builders are often frustrated and disappointed. They really want their leaders to make a !#@$* decision and develop a plan! Provide a forum to share ideas, value team opinions and input, and mentor them to grow as valued parts of the team.

THE JOY SUCKERS—naysayers, neggies, pessimists, and other downer individuals who see only the dark cloud, never the silver lining. When a team shows improvement, they find a way to bring them down. No celebrating. They are never satisfied. Nothing is ever enough. No one is ever worthy. As such, they do not reward and find it extremely difficult to give even perfunctory praise.

THE INCOGNITOS—invisible persons who are leaders in title only, not in physical presence or involvement. This leadership approach has pros and cons. Pro: you don't have someone hovering over you while you work. Con: it is difficult to get direction. These leaders empower their teams to a fault. Imagine being cut loose and allowed to float around in outer space. But watch out when Incognitos return to action. They come back with hurricane force. When they find things not to their liking, they yell, scream, and threaten to make drastic procedural and personnel changes. I heard someone describe this as "Pigeon Management." They come in, crap all over everyone, and fly away. The good news is that they're gone in a couple days.

THE MICROMANAGERS—those who lead at a far more detailed level than is necessary or appropriate. These folks are the definition of "anal retentive" and relentlessly review the work done in their departments, tweaking even the smallest things. They constantly "check in" with their team. They want an accounting of every minute of time and feedback on everything being done. They'd probably like a full report of restroom breaks if the law allowed. In essence, micromanagers are control freaks who trust no one—not even their own team and possibly themselves.

Nothing makes teams feel more worthless, more incompetent and more ambivalent about their work than a micromanager. I'm speaking from experience. I once worked for a leader who wanted an accounting of my calls each day. I found myself depressed and beginning to doubt my ability. At that point, I stood up for myself and left the company. Unfortunately, many salespeople put up with their micromanager and live their lives with someone chipping away at their already low self-esteem and diminished confidence, which eventually leads to low performance. If you want your team to be unsuccessful, doubt them—it works every time.

THE NARCISSISTS—self-absorbed people who always shift the focus to themselves ("But enough about you, let's talk about me!"). Never forget that the people you are leading want to talk about their careers and work, not yours. As a leader, you are to guide, motivate, and nurture them, not vice versa.

THE UNDERMINERS—leaders who talk behind their team members' backs and set them up for failure. Their passive-aggressive behavior will have you spinning. Get out—they will only make you crazier than you already are.

THE YELLERS AND SCREAMERS—in short, the ones who throw adult tantrums. In these cases, ask yourself: Would that behavior be acceptable at Microsoft or any successful organization? Get out fast!

Enough with the bad and the ugly leadership types and their shortcomings. The real role of leaders is twofold: First and foremost, they must truly lead the people in their organizations, generating revenue and providing excellent customer service. Second, they must mentor their teams to help them grow, both personally and professionally. If one of your team members accepts a better position—inside or outside the company—don't look at it as a setback. View it as a positive sign that you have succeeded in your job as a leader, that you helped develop a competent, sought-after individual. In contrast, leaders who do not allow their teams to grow personally and professionally impair their organization, resulting in chaos, low productivity and negativism.

Great leaders keep abreast of new leadership styles. They take courses and read books on how to better guide their teams. They are good communicators and find it easy to praise their team members. They motivate with a kind word and empower their people by merely believing in them. They allow mistakes to be tools for learning and guide their people to success.

How do you know if you are a good leader? Prepare a presentation or simply write down leadership styles you use and how you might explain them to a group of new leaders. A successful leader can do it in a heartbeat. They understand the process. A good rule of thumb is: If you can't write a leadership course, it's time to take one.

Chapter Takeaway:

CHAPTER 7 | FINDING SHIRLEY

Find what motivates you and success will follow

When I first went into sales, what I wanted most was to earn more than Shirley, the sister of my boyfriend. Shirley was a radiology technician. She earned a nice living and I got really tired of hearing about it. I knew the right sales position could easily catapult me over Shirley's salary and her yearly cost-of-living raise. I hoped that would silence my boyfriend's constant reminders of Shirley's success. I was jealous and finally had a way to rid myself of the jealousy in a positive way.

My parents thought I was crazy when I quit my $25,000-a-year administrative assistant job and took a sales position that paid me $200 and a tank of gas each week, plus commissions. Within three years, I was earning $100,000 a year—a great deal more than the successful Shirley, who became a non-factor anyway after my breakup with her brother.

To motivate your salespeople, you need to find their "Shirleys." Find out what drives their hunger for success. Talk to them, then really listen—most salespeople like to talk, and eventually they'll reveal what makes them tick.

Motivating Factors

Salespeople usually want recognition and respect in the companies and industries they serve. To them, a good gauge of their success is when they can get a new job in the industry without a résumé because their excellent reputation precedes them.

Some salespeople want to move into leadership to train new salespeople, oversee sales and marketing projects, and so on. A good salesperson is not necessarily a good leader, however, and some who make the switch soon realize their error and switch back. From a business perspective, be sure to think twice before letting your top salesperson leave that role for leadership.

Most of all, I have noticed that successful salespeople want more than life's essentials. They enjoy the opportunity to make a comfortable living for themselves and their families. Some want to purchase real estate, others like nice clothing or expensive cars, and still others want to travel. I have yet to meet the successful salesperson who hoards their earnings. Salespeople certainly can be charitably inclined, but sales is a career that allows one to give and then replenish the pot.

I wasn't motivated by expensive cars, vacations or nice clothes. I simply wanted to be as successful as Shirley. That goal led me to a sales career because I knew it would put me in control of my own destiny. Being a commissioned salesperson, I would never again have to endure a yearly review, hear someone else's version of my success, then get a token cost-of-living raise regardless. Instead I would be compensated for my productivity—I could become as successful as I wanted to be based on my own performance, like golf.

Most people go into sales because they want that direct benefit between effort and earnings. It's puzzling that so few companies seem to realize and act upon this nearly universal reality.

Demotivating Factors

A salesperson with hunter instincts is hungry for success, both personally and professionally. But many companies have compensation structures that work against those instincts, limiting their sales team's productivity.

When a company lacks a structured bonus plan for its sales team, the hunters drift into the farmer mode. They become comfortable in their chairs and in their offices, discussing lunch plans with colleagues instead of scheduling lunches with customers and prospects. Once they get comfortable in their desk chairs, getting them back to capturing new business is like moving a mountain.

Small to mid-sized companies tend to favor what I call the "What Have You Done for Me Lately?" compensation package. They put their salespeople on salary and award an arbitrary bonus here and there. The perspective in these companies is that the teams are lucky to have their jobs and they should be grateful when the leaders choose to share the wealth. This type of leadership seems unable to grasp that when thecommissioned salesperson is making great money, so is the company. Do the math, keeping in mind that the new wave of talented and confident salespeople won't stay in these situations for long. They're hungry and they'll go where they are recognized, appreciated and compensated for producing.

Too much money can be another demotivating factor—in particular, when companies pay their salespeople too much base salary. The salespeople get comfortable on that salary and have no incentive to move forward. They just tread water until they're asked to leave or they stay on as the company's "good soldiers." These people might have some value to their companies, but like a savings account, the return on the company's investment is low. These companies don't realize that a salesperson is often driven by a low initial salary—just enough to get by—with hopes of reaping great rewards from great effort. Thus my $200 a week salary and a tank of gas entry into sales.

Structuring Success

It is up to the leadership team to build a creative, structured and consistent way to   motivate and compensate its salespeople. You can't talk, coach, beat or threaten them into success, but you can show them what their success can bring. With the right program in place, the sales department will flourish. Every month won't be a winner, but the goal is to win 8 of every 12.

A great way to grow a business and keep salespeople focused is to base their compensation on individual quarterly productivity. I'm a big fan of plans that have no real cap on what a salesperson can earn. Instead, they set the base salary at a level where the salespeople can live, but not flourish, then let them build from there.

I work with companies that have yearly intern programs and they know it's in their best interests to offer the interns a chance to boost their salary by working on commission or earning bonuses. This type of compensation structure offers interns the opportunity to have some control of their income and measure their success while enabling the company to identify and prove future full-timers.

Rewarding salespeople based on their profitability gives them an incentive to close only profitable business. They increase their compensation to attain their own personal goals—whatever their "Shirley" might be—and the company enjoys a strong bottom line.

I once worked with a salesperson who had great sales skills, but he was not reaching his numbers quarter after quarter. The company owners had an excellent compensation program in place and were baffled. Seeing his potential, I encouraged the company to keep him. No matter how many times they wanted to let him go, I was confident of his talent.

A year or so after the training program, I heard from one of the owners that he was doing well and was now their top salesperson. It seems his wife quit her high-paying job to stay home with their new son. That was the incentive he needed to boost his productivity—he had found his "Shirley."

Chapter Takeaway:

_____

_____

_____

CHAPTER 8 | THE POWER OF A PLAN

Set strategic goals and others will see the vision

Imagine you're sitting at an airport, but you have no ticket, no destination, and no real direction of any kind. How would you feel? Probably confused, lost, frustrated, and resigned, among other things. Without a destination, there's no reason for you to be at the airport in the first place, unless you're picking up your cousin Vinny from Ashtabula, Ohio (really, that's where my relatives are from).

Now imagine that your company has no plan—no target, only darts that have no way of knowing whether they've hit the bullseye or made another aimless hole in the wall. How would your teams feel? Probably like they're in an airport without a destination. That's why it's so important to have a game plan. In sports, the team with the best game plan usually wins. It's the same for your company and teams.

I'll admit that some companies—the exceptions—can prosper without a plan. They inherently grow year after year thanks to a talented visionary or strong teams who know how to achieve success informally, almost instinctively. However, too many companies operate with on-the-fly, day-to-day leadership. The problem with that approach is no one in the company really knows where they are going. Aimless movement.

Companies with a plan align themselves for success. These companies have a destination each and every year and that destination includes "meeting our numbers." Leadership has executed the team-building skills learned during training sessions and the competition has no idea what they are up to until they see the result.

Successful or not, when companies don't have a plan, leaders often desire more without really knowing what "more" means. The team is like a hamster on a wheel—it's running, running, running, but with no real endpoint in mind. Under these circumstances, leaders can ride the teams month after month, week after week. There might be a sporadic burst of success. But these anxious teams spend so much time avoiding the leader's wrath that they become "pleasers" rather than professionals. They become reactive rather than proactive. This ultimately leads them to a place where they don't particularly like themselves. If you're a leader who feels you must ride or badger your people to motivate them, you have the wrong people. If you feel strongly that you have the right people, you have the wrong leadership style.

I speak from experience when I say that sales careers can be exhausting when the company does not have a plan in place. If you're a leader, ask yourself: Do I have my people running and jumping aimlessly, or do I give them specific destinations? Have I provided them with room for growth in their careers? How can I help them get there?

If you're a salesperson, ask your sales leader where he or she wants you to be at the end of the year and then go for it. If you don't, you're essentially in a race with no finish line. Beware of the boss who doesn't give you a clear understanding of what he or she considers success. You won't know if you reach it and will never know where you stand. You'll be playing in a game without a lineup, with the rules changing every inning. There's no way to win in that scenario. Every Monday when you get to work, the furniture has been rearranged and you have to learn how to navigate your office all over again. Sound familiar?

Now is the time to stop the madness, step off the treadmill, and examine the whole concept of planning for your company. All businesses should have several different kinds of plans in place that correspond to various aspects of the business. Start with an overall strategic plan—include cash flow forecasts; marketing strategies, sales, technology and operational plans, management, leadership and administration plans, and expenditure projections, among others. The point is that you need some kind of plan or direction to bring clarity and vision to virtually every area of your business.

Even the best leaders sometimes forget about succession plans. If you're a company owner and have no "if-I-fell-off-the-earth" plan for your firm, you're basically leaving your family to slug it out with the employees, relatives and the lawyers. If you don't already have a succession plan, start thinking about one.

To get started in creating a plan of any kind for your company, consider these questions:

- Do I have a clear definition of what constitutes success?
- Am I taking my business or department toward that success proactively, or am I just in the business of reacting?
- Do I set clear goals and timelines for myself and my teams?
- Do all our people know their value?
- Have I developed a succession plan to protect my family, employees and stockholders?
- Do I feel, at times, like I'm running in place? If so, why do I feel this way? What can I do to address this feeling?

Who can help you prepare a plan? You can certainly enlist your team for input, especially those affected directly. Research shows that people have greater "buy in" to plans they help create as opposed to plans foisted on them from above.

For plans requiring more professional expertise, you can hire management consultants or attorneys experienced in succession planning. Make sure they're highly qualified and are recommended, ideally by a colleague who has first-hand knowledge of their qualifications.

Once you have a plan, you need leaders who are willing and able to execute it. They must be committed to the plan's measurable implementation. Good leaders know it takes teamwork to run their company or department. The best ideas don't have to be their own. They know how to give credit where it is due. They don't count hours, they count successes. They lead effectively by using timelines and measurements to track progress.

When a company develops a plan and finds success, it doesn't stop—it takes its performance up a notch each year. If you want to alleviate the stress of not knowing where you're going, develop a plan. You can't afford to be sitting around—in an airport or in your business—without a destination, even if it's Ashtabula.

Chapter Takeaway:

_____

_____

_____

CHAPTER 9 | LEGENDARY CUSTOMER SERVICE

The foundation of a strong company

Customer service—good or bad—is the stuff of legend. Who hasn't heard the (untrue) tale of the Neiman Marcus cookie: A woman enjoys a chocolate-chip cookie at the department store's café and asks the chef for the recipe. The chef says it will cost "two-fifty," and later she finds a $250 charge on her credit-card statement that the company refuses to refund. She gets revenge by emailing the recipe to everyone she knows.

Conversely, a legend about Nordstrom reinforces the company's customer-service reputation. As the story goes, a man walks into a Nordstrom with a set of tires and tells the clerk he'd like to return them for a refund. Even though Nordstrom has never sold tires, the clerk asks him how much he paid, opens the register, and gives him the refund.

Research shows people spread word of bad customer experiences more widely than the good. You might think your service is exceptional because you give customers what they want. That's a reactive approach, and it results in adequate service. Truly good service is proactive—delivered by someone who anticipates what customers might want and giving it to them before they can even think of it themselves.

Customer Service Basics

Customers are not only those who buy products or services from your company. Though external customers are very important, a company cannot get anything done if the internal customers—the people working together in the business—are unhappy. Use the same strategies whether the person you're assisting is in the next office or on another continent.

Start with the basics: All customers expect and deserve active listening and questioning, good intentions, and empathy. They want you to be friendly and fair and they want control of the situation, which you can give them by offering options or alternatives. They want you to follow through on your promises with prompt action.

How can a customer tell if you have good intentions, empathy, and friendliness? Often it's not what you say, it's how you say it. About 55 percent of what we learn about others comes from body language; 38 percent comes from voice tone, speed, and inflection; and only 7 percent comes from the actual words spoken. I test this with my dog Jamba by standing in front of him, smiling and telling him in a sing-song voice that he is the ugliest dog I have ever seen. He gets very excited and wags his tail because for Jamba, body language and tone are almost all he understands. This works with babies, too, but think twice before you call someone's baby ugly, even if you do it in a happy, smiling way. It seems to anger parents who are within earshot.

In the presence of a customer, good body language means eye contact, positive body language, focus, a neat appearance, and respect for the customer's personal space.

Out-of-Sight Service

That's great, you might say, but we conduct most of our business over the phone, email or text. Believe it or not, body language is important in those interactions as well. When someone smiles while talking on the phone or sending an electronic correspondence, the smile can be heard. Just a side note: Someone sitting up straight sounds better than someone slouching, too.

Tone and inflection take on even greater importance in phone interactions. Try this exercise: Say: "Please take out the garbage" three different ways, and emphasize a different word each time. See how the tone changes? If you don't understand tone, spend a few days with a teenager or a sarcastic adult—someone who can give a word like "OK" a dozen different inflections, not to mention several interpretations of body language.

The person answering the phone is the caller's first impression of your company. Train teams about phone rules and expectations: how many rings are acceptable before someone answers, what the person answering the phone should say, and how to speak with the customers. Simple courtesies, such as using the customer's name during the conversation and avoiding slang, can help a team develop rapport with a customer over the phone.

When I'm training people, I recommend they offer different options to the callers. For example, "Joe is unavailable right now, would you like to leave a message on his voice mail?" Most people will say "yes", but some might want to speak with someone else, and others might want to send an email instead. You don't know unless you ask. That's a much more customer-friendly strategy than just saying, "hold on" and transferring the call right into the dreaded and unwanted voice mail.

A company that does business primarily by email might want to have additional rules for that medium. Email takes away the cues people get from body language and tone, so it's especially important that the words are clear and unambiguous. Good manners and good grammar are as important in an email as they are in person and on the phone. While I love texting, I believe it should only be used with those you know well and for the right reasons. Texting a thank you is not enough. Always follow up with a written note.

Responding to Complaints

Even with good service, things can go wrong. You might miss a deadline, deliver the wrong product, or miss a follow up. The customer might be unhappy with your product or feel he has been treated unfairly. If the customer complains, be appreciative of the feedback. Most people don't bother, they just take their business elsewhere. A company might never know that there's been a problem until it's too late. If you get the wrong pizza more than once, most people will order from another pizza joint rather than call and complain.

Not every customer complaint is valid, however, and there is a time to draw the line. Often, the problems come from the same customers over and over, who make requests that get harder and harder to accommodate. It becomes clear that they are just abusing the process. Do your teams know at what point they should say "no," or how to communicate that gracefully? This is an aspect of customer service training that most companies neglect.

When I provide customer service training, I work with the leadership team to identify the company's service flaws and replace them with good manners and clear procedures. When you realize that it takes five times more energy, resources and money to get a new customer than it does to maintain a current one, one might decide such training is worth the investment.

Chapter Takeaway:

CHAPTER 10 | DON'T BE JUST ANOTHER FRUITCAKE

Tips for giving and partying professionally during the holiday season

When the holidays approach, sales teams gear up for what can be the busiest and most exhausting time of the year. It can be hard to sustain holiday cheer when you're simultaneously trying to meet year-end goals, schedule time for your family and friends, and make your customers feel special. By putting a little bit of thought into two standards of celebration—presents and parties—you can ensure you make a positive impression on your clients and prospects and not come across as stale, unwelcome, and boozy as a holiday fruitcake.

The Perfect Present

Long before the holiday season, marketing departments begin trying to figure out the ideal gift for sales teams to deliver to their valued customers. Over the years I have seen a myriad of gift types, from the proverbial fruitcake to charitable donations made in the customer's name. I'm sorry to say that almost everything has been done, and nothing much stands out anymore. All those breakfasts, lunches, dinners and cheese-popcorn tins blend together giving our customers high cholesterol and an expansion notch on their belt when all the hubbub is over. Even if a company has a brilliant idea for a gift one year, it often finds that creativity hard to sustain the next.

Perhaps true originality comes not from what you give, but when. I learned from a friend's manufacturing company to celebrate with customers at Thanksgiving, giving thanks for another year of their business. This act made my company stand out—and I doubt the customers expect another helping during December. Being a holiday early bird frees the sales team to plan the very important December visits, enjoy the holiday season, and prepare for the New Year by setting goals and the strategies for attaining them. It's also a time when the competition is busy delivering fruitcakes. Just food for thought if you are trying to pick off some of their business.

Partying Professionally

Even though December brings fewer daylight hours, workdays begin to extend long into the night with trade association, company and customer parties. Newbies especially wonder about business party etiquette: What do I wear? What do I bring? How do I behave? When in doubt, be professional and you can never go wrong.

The trickiest issue often is alcohol. Err on the side of caution whenever alcohol is served. If you're the host for a party, dinner, lunch, or even breakfast, you're responsible for ensuring your guests get home safely. You never want to hear that a valued customer suffered in any way due to excessive celebrating at your event. Why create a bad memory? Take care of your customers like you would your own kids.

Even when you're not hosting, be aware of how alcohol and "holiday cheer" can affect the behavior of coworkers, customers and friends. If you're worried about what you might say or do, stay sober. If you're worried about the behavior of others, slip out before the nonsense begins. Avoid becoming the topic of post-party gossip. And if the post-party gossip starts making its way around the water cooler, steer clear.

Appropriate attire depends on the occasion and setting. My basic rule is, don't wear anything less than you would wear to your grandmother's funeral. (This rule doesn't apply if your grandmother is or was a biker.) In other words, dress to respect the hosts.

Men can always wear a dark suit and tie, then remove the tie if they feel overdressed. Women have more of a challenge. It takes too much time and dexterity to pluck the sequins off a dress one by one to make it basic black. When in doubt, simply call and ask about the attire. A business suit is always appropriate.

Much to my chagrin, some professional women tend to dress provocatively at holiday business events. Is that the image you want to present? Certainly men don't veer towards this choice. You'll end up with customers or coworkers who are thinking more about what you're wearing than what you're saying. I prefer to present myself as personable, funny, and interesting, and personally blame these women as the reason women earn less for the same work as men.

Networking No-Nos

Arriving fashionably late is a faux pas at a business function. As a matter of fact, it's best to arrive early and get the lay of the land. Most networking gurus suggest positioning yourself somewhere between the entrance and the buffet. I always prefer to be near the beverage station (nice way to say "bar"), as most attendees make it over there at some point during the evening.

Not everyone has the ability to work the room, but anyone can be personable. That means saying hello when someone makes eye contact. Practice this behavior on people you see while shopping or walking down the street. If you see someone you think you know at an event, approach that person and ask: "Have we met before?" If you are mistaken, no harm, no foul. Now you know someone new.

Make sure your handshake is acceptable as well. A good, firm handshake is important for both men and women. You would be surprised at how many executives have a really weak handshake. Aim for something stronger than a limp fish and not so strong that the person winces in pain.

Remember that a party—especially someone else's party—is not a contest to meet as many people as you can. Bring your business cards, but be selective about handing them out. You don't want to look like the obnoxious salesperson who attends a function just for the networking, even if it's true.

If you do make a few good contacts, follow up immediately with a letter or note card. Why use such a slow form of communication? Because people can easily delete a phone message, email or text. Handwritten notes sit around for a while. And besides, a handwritten note makes it look like you went the extra mile and makes you stand out in a positive way among your peers and competition.

'Tis the season to see your customers, get the pulse of the industry, ask for leads, and spread some cheer. Make the time you spend away from friends and family worth your while by meeting new people and behaving professionally. Otherwise, like a fruitcake, you might become just another holiday joke.

Chapter Takeaway:

CHAPTER 11 | ARE YOU SETTING GOALS OR SETTING WISHES?

A step-by-step guide to making success a reality instead of a pipedream

January is named for the Roman mythological figure of Janus, the god of beginnings and endings. He's usually portrayed as having two faces, one looking to the year ahead and one looking back at the year just ended. The start of the New Year is always a good time to look in those two directions, to review last year's goals and to write some new ones. Looking back, did you surpass your goals, meet your mark or fall short? Looking ahead, are you setting the same goals every year, or are you continuously challenging yourself?

Working without goals is like building a skyscraper without a set of plans. They're essential for success, but they're just the first step. Goals mean nothing without plans and target dates. A goal without a target is not a goal; it is a wish. I know some people who were born into success, but none who have wished themselves there. You achieve your goals with strategies—and time management. Without a target date, even clear goals with strategies can slide.

I'll walk you through the goal-setting journey of someone I'll call Joe Sales, who asked me to help him set goals. The first draft of Joe's sales goals looked like this:

• Increase sales
• Achieve 100-percent retention
• Take a leadership course
• Get a promotion

His goals were a good start—at least Joe knew what he wanted. But they were too broad and had no target dates or benchmarks. So I worked with Joe to better define each of those goals. I had him consider the six fundamental questions—who, what, when, where, why, and how—for each goal. For example, how will he increase sales, and by how much? What can he do to improve account retention? What leadership courses will he take, where, why and completed by when? How will he pay for the course? What type of advancement does he have in mind? What are his opportunities for growth within his firm? Who plays a role in deciding his advancement? By thinking through such questions, Joe came up with a detailed set of strategies and target dates to add to his original goals.

Increase sales

- Obtain one "A" type of account per quarter and four or five "B" types of accounts per quarter
- Work on profitable sales margins on all accounts
- Ask for leads regularly from current customer base
- Join an industry organization and become active on a committee by (set a date)
- Cultivate respect and influential relationships within that organization
- Develop plan to call on my customers
- Spend at least two hours a week making calls for new business
- Schedule a minimum of three sales calls a week
- Develop both internal and external relationships to enhance customer service
- Buy lunch for support team quarterly
- Give compliments and thanks to both internal and external customers, both in person and through notecards
- Be the person others want to help
- Use customer relationship system (CRM) to document all customer contact

Take a leadership course

- Identify my leadership strengths and weaknesses
- Work with my company to select appropriate training
- Take at least two courses this year
- Read at least four leadership books this year

Get a promotion

- Discuss with leadership my desire for advancement
- Identify what skills I need to be considered for leadership
- Find out where I fit in my company's mission and goals and how I can assist the company in achieving its goals
- Keep an ear to the ground for leadership opportunities or restructuring
- Meet quarterly with leadership and offer to take on additional responsibilities

Once you set goals and strategies for achieving them, review goals at least monthly. If you have a mentor, ask that person to hold you accountable for meeting your targets. This is especially important if your supervisor or company doesn't require them. For years I set goals that no one really saw. It was a point of pride for me to have goals, even if no one else knew about them. But it's far more enjoyable to have someone to acknowledge it when you reach your goals. And you should always reward yourself when you meet a goal. That's how I ended up buying myself a condo in one of Chicago's trendy neighborhoods.

There are other rewards for setting and achieving goals. Looking at Joe's goals, I suspect he will benefit financially from meeting them because the company for which he works gives out performance-based bonuses. Improving his interactions with his colleagues and customers will most likely bring him respect in his department and firm. By furthering his education and his understanding of the company, he will become a better candidate for promotion should the opportunity arise. He will stand out rather than just blend in.

I believe leadership is on the horizon for Joe Sales because he isn't expecting someone to just give him a higher position; he's working to earn it. When he does begin to lead, the goals he set and the strategies he used to achieve them will have positioned him well. The leadership team will respect his determination and strategy; his peers will admire his commitment to furthering his education and his sales success; and others in the company will appreciate the gratitude he has shown them for their contributions to his success and to the firm.

At the end of the year, I'll meet with Joe to discuss which goals he accomplished and which he did not. We'll set new goals and tweak some of the carry-overs. I know, for instance, that he has enrolled in only one leadership course, even though his company has approved a second one. He never put a specific date on when he would get the additional training and it fell through the cracks. It happens, but we'll set new target dates, put reminders in his calendar, and create a new goal to stay on task.

Chapter Takeaway:

CHAPTER 12 | BEWARE OF BAD APPLES

The truth in how one can spoil the rest of the bunch

In a previous chapter, I examined bad leadership behavior so it's only fair that I turn the spotlight this time on teams and, specifically, the "bad apples." My goal is to improve how you deal with these toxic types. Such people consume more of your time than you have to give and, ultimately, they either leave or get fired.

We've all heard that one rotten apple can spoil the whole barrel—and it's true. Anyone who has owned a business or leads a team can share with you a story about a bad apple or two. The bad apple can create chaos in a department or even throughout the company. Even the best teams can be affected by bad apples and, before you know it, the whole damn bushel is tainted.

The best way to avoid bad apples is to not hire them in the first place. That requires a thorough, thoughtful interviewing process. Unfortunately, it's common for untrained interviewers to do most of the talking, enabling the bad apple to slip into the company by merely being polite. Your questions must allow the interviewee to speak and you must check their references carefully.

Thorough interviewing is critical whether you're talking with totally unknown applicants or candidates who have been referred to you. On the surface, such referrals are a nice, well-meaning gesture. People like to help people. When you refer someone, you help two people—the jobseeker and the employer. I like to refer people, but I always specify how I know the person I'm referring just in case it doesn't work out. I've made some excellent referrals for key positions through networking. (I've even introduced a few couples, who subsequently married, including a close friend and my sister who both married customers of mine.) Don't forget, though, such referrals are just an introduction. You, the employer, should still ask your contact a few questions about the referred person. Some questions you might ask are:

- Why do you think the person would be a good fit for my company?
- Have you ever done business with the person in the past?
- Why is the recommended person looking for a new position?
- When you met him/her, what was your first impression?

Asking such questions is part of being thorough and it shows you're taking the necessary time to make a smart hire. Many times, employers need to fill an immediate need and rush their hiring decision. Remember the old saying that haste makes waste? Well, it's true. When you don't have the necessary interviewing skills or don't take enough time, you'll hire the wrong people.

What happens if you're approached by someone from the competition for a position in your company? Your first reaction might be to hire them immediately because, after all, you wouldn't have to train them since they already know the business and they may even bring a customer base with them. Sounds like a no-brainer. But be careful (unless, of course, you solicited the person yourself). Some competitors' teams may simply think the grass is greener elsewhere and they may have unrealistic expectations about how much better it would be to work for your firm. So don't be too anxious. Get the whole story. Job jumpers are just that.

Once again, it's crucial to ask the right questions before hiring. For instance, consider asking any applicant from a competitor:

- What makes you want to leave your current company?
- What attracted you to apply at our company?
- If you begin working here and then decide to return to any of your former employers, would they hire you back?
- What are your career goals and how would our company assist you in achieving them?

So, let's assume you innocently and unwittingly hire a bad apple. What can you do? First, make sure your company has a probationary period for all new hires. After a set number of probationary days (try to keep it under the unemployment requirements), you can then make a more informed decision whether to keep the person.

Unfortunately, the bad apple will often know unemployment laws, workers comp laws, and any other laws they need to work the system. Rules of thumb from my personal experience:

- If an applicant focuses on insurance, sick days and vacation in the interview, he may be a bad apple.
- If an employee takes a day off in the first 30 days and it's the Monday after the Super Bowl, she may be a bad apple.
- If a truck driver rams your truck into a garage door the week after he's hired and leaves the scene of the accident, chances are he's a bad apple.
- If an employee reveals that she believes she's the mother of Jesus (true story) over lunch one day, she may be a bad (or crazy) apple.

One problem with probationary periods is they must end. This creates opportunity for bad apples who are adept at not showing their true colors immediately. They can be on their best behavior a certain amount of time, then—watch out!—the chaos begins. And once it starts, it's like a tornado as it moves though the company.

You can't imagine the time you'll expend dealing with bad apples—disciplining them, listening to how unhappy they are and how unfairly they're being treated. Are they worth all this time? Of course not. You could put those hours to better use by focusing on your team players. And will the bad apples continue to drive you crazy? Of course. As a leadership expert once observed, "The person you fire is not the person who drives you crazy."

So what are you to do? My main advice is to document all bad-apple incidents. That way, when they leave or are asked to leave, your company will have the necessary information to fight whatever claims they may bring against you. Don't try to change them and don't give them too many chances. While I believe in second chances, no one is worth the third, fifth and seventh chances.

Chapter Takeaway:

_____

_____

_____

CHAPTER 13 | THE POWER OF MENTORING

Find one, be one, reap the rewards

If you stopped people on the street and asked them to define mentor, they'd probably say it means a wise and loyal adviser or, more casually, a teacher or coach. (Or you would get a blank stare immediately letting you know they don't know what that means). In Greek mythology, Mentor was the name of the loyal friend and adviser of Ulysses—the guy who went on the Odyssey—and teacher of his son, Telemachus. So, as you can see, the whole mentoring thing goes back a long way.

Then, as now, there are three aspects to mentoring: You can find a mentor who will help guide you through your life and/or career; you can become a mentor yourself; or you can do both. Though it might seem like you'd learn more from having a mentor than being one, I've found that mentoring relationships can greatly benefit both people involved.

Finding a Mentor

More often than not, mentors are simply people whom you admire and try to emulate in your career. How to choose a mentor all boils down to what's important to you. Are you looking for someone who has reached a certain level of success, has traits you would like to learn or inherit, has a degree of power you seek, or has a leadership style you admire or knowledge you value? Those are all ways to choose a mentor.

My first mentor was the man I worked for as a secretary right out of high school. Ray was a general agent for 13 salespeople at a life insurance company. I liked his style of setting goals and assisting his reps in attaining them. He never took credit for his "assists," and he shared his victories (he actually received a bonus for his own performance and shared it with his team). He hired the company's first black and first female sales representatives. He was an ex-Marine with tattoos on his forearms and he was still giving me orders up to a month before he died. I followed his lead every time. Ray always had my best interests in mind and it was a great feeling having him guide me through my sales and business career. There are still many moments when I wish he were here to take my call.

Mentors pop up in all corners of your life. We have mentors in raising families, spiritual mentors, even a mentor who teaches you how to lighten up— mentors of joy! A mentor can help in any area of your life in which you'd like to improve. Even businessmen I dated in my single days mentored me in what it takes to run my own business. Those years were both painful and useful.

Being a Mentor

When it comes to being a mentor, you can't just tell someone, "I want to be your mentor" or worse, "I am your mentor." You cannot assign your own self to this task. Mentoring is about respect. In fact, you might be someone's mentor and not even know it.

For example, I was surprised and flattered to be invited to the small wedding of a female coworker. In the receiving line, I introduced my husband and myself to the bride's mother, who said, "I'm so glad to meet our daughter's mentor." Hearing those words made my day. I enjoyed working with this bright young woman, who had earned two master's degrees by the age of 23. She often confided in me and I'm glad I was able to help her. We lost touch after her marriage and even with social media, I can't seem to locate her. (Her name is Tuesdae. If you know someone by that name, let her know I am looking for her.)

If you're a helpful and knowledgeable leader, you're probably a mentor. If you're successful in your career and humble about your achievements, you're probably a mentor. If anyone looks up to your good—and, unfortunately, even bad—behaviors, you're a mentor. If you run on an even keel, more than likely, you are a mentor. There are ways to establish more formal mentoring relationships, too. If you would like to volunteer your services, many business associations, high schools and colleges offer mentoring programs that pair you with students or new professionals who are interested in pursuing a career in your field.

Over a decade ago, I signed up for a mentoring program at a local high school that paired me with a student interested in marketing. Because sales and marketing are always lumped together, so were Katie and I. We met a few times at events the high school sponsored. I could tell Katie was different from the other students: She wore a business suit to the planned business meetings and her manners were impeccable. We didn't have much of a chance to get to know each other, though, because the events didn't give us much one-on-one time. But at the end of the year, the program organizers ask the mentors to take their student protégés to work with them. Katie and I spent an entire day together and really clicked. We weren't necessarily alike, but we developed a respect for each other. Katie is now a successful marketing professional. I love watching her grow both personally and professionally.

Reaping the Rewards

In my career, I've been fortunate to reap the benefits of being mentored and serving as a mentor. I still keep in touch with my mentors and now I'm in a position to assist them from time to time. What were once mentoring relationships have turned into close and supportive friendships. Recently, I did a training session and one of my mentors was in attendance. A little unnerving, but rewarding when his comments were favorable.

I've also encouraged others to learn the different sides of mentoring. For instance, I directed a youth choir at my church. When younger children joined the choir, I paired them with older children whom they call their mentors. A couple of years later, these children became the mentors of the younger children and so on.

We never know who might be looking for a mentor so we should live our lives by setting positive examples and assisting others whenever and wherever we can. And if people have mentored you in the past, tell them. They will be flattered and it might even make their day.

Chapter Takeaway:

CHAPTER 14 | THE RISKS OF ROLLER-COASTER LEADERSHIP

Finding the right side of consistency

As a teenager, I worked as a clerk in a clothing store. I answered to assistant management personnel and they answered to the store manager who managed more than 20 stores. They worked long hours, spending most of the time on their feet and providing leadership and customer service to everyone who entered the store. Unfortunately, I didn't appreciate their efforts until I was in a leadership role myself.

On a typical day, a leader answers calls, meets with his or her team, attends meetings, does paperwork, visits with customers, and puts out fires. Good leaders don't allow these crises to color interactions with their team. In fact, these leaders praise, validate, and consistently encourage their teams to achieve while insulating them from the sometimes-wild fluctuations of their own milieu.

The Pluses of Praise

Praise is like that old joke about voting in Chicago: it works best if done early and often. Teams need frequent praise for their efforts. Everybody likes to receive praise, but some leaders cannot find it in themselves to offer it. They deliver praise so rarely that cobwebs are attached to any complimentary words leaving their lips. But wise leaders who regularly use praise to develop their teams tell you how they get as much satisfaction as the people they are leading. Positive responses to praise are inevitable.

Validation is another valuable strategy for empowering workers. How does a leader validate his or her teams? By acknowledging their ideas, efforts, and goals. Such acknowledgement is a sign of respect and value.

Validation goes hand in hand with listening. When a team member approaches a leader with an idea, good or bad, the leader recognizes an opportunity to create a positive experience through listening, validating, and building on it. I learned this during my improv days as part of the "Yes…and" exercise used to help improvisers agree and move the action forward.

Even-Steven

Perhaps the only thing worse than never praising or validating teams is doing it inconsistently. Leadership expects the same or better performance from their workers every day. Teams want the same kind of daily consistency from their leaders, especially when it involves feedback on their work efforts. Regrettably, some leaders are more like Dr. Jekyll and Mr. Hyde, bringing their teams along with them to experience the dizzying effects of their split personality. This results in having teams and companies who are hesitant and uncertain because they don't know which personality will show up.

I remember one evening when the president of a company went out to dinner with his sales team to celebrate a banner year of profit and growth. Everyone enjoyed the celebration and went home happy and positive about the company and their individual contributions. The next day, the same president arrives to work in a foul mood. Perhaps his morning was off to a bad start: he left home late, was snarled in traffic, his cell phone died—any number of things. When he entered the office, heads started rolling! He barked at everyone who approached him and created an atmosphere of tension and confusion. His inconsistent behavior neutralized all the enthusiasm and confidence shared during the previous night's celebration dinner.

Some teams report receiving a bonus one week, then having their productivity challenged the next. It's possible the company's circumstances changed in the interim, but that's not what is communicated. Instead, the teams hear, "Last week you were doing great. That level of performance this week is inadequate." Such a message is not merely inconsistent; it's confusing and cruel.

Sadly, this type of leadership is the norm. I believe poor leadership is one of the hardest things to change at a company and when not addressed can cripple leaders and cultures. Owning or operating a company has its highs and lows, but owners and leaders need to insulate workers from that roller-coaster ride when it's not relevant to their work.

Achieving Consistency

Medication and therapy can help smooth out serious personality swings, but perhaps all you need is to be consistent and put things in perspective. I've found books and articles about servant leadership to be valuable. There are many to choose from.

We've all seen examples of people overreacting to small setbacks. I remember when my son's seventh-grade basketball team was getting crushed by a rival middle school. The mother of another boy on our team couldn't bear to watch the game and she kept commenting on her despair. She asked why I was so detached and unconcerned about the game's outcome. I politely told her that my uncle had just been diagnosed with lung cancer. There are life-altering experiences and there's the everyday stuff. Sort it out and react accordingly. (That woman avoided me thereafter).

That perspective is equally valuable in the workplace. Misplace your cell phone? It's an annoyance, sure, but don't take it out on your team. Even a bigger setback, like losing a big account, needs to remain in perspective. Your team must know you won't overreact to every piece of bad news—or they might just stop telling you things that could upset you and the company never learns what to correct.

Unlearning Bad Habits

Unfortunately, some leaders believe erratic and inconsistent behavior is effective. They develop their leadership styles by observing their predecessors instead of learning how to be an effective leader within their own unique personality. This can be a particular problem in a family business. There was a time when simply growing up in the business was good enough, but those days are long gone. Today, the worst thing parents can do to their children is pass along the family business without equipping them with the education and training needed to survive in today's competitive business environment.

As a teenager working at the clothing store, I learned something from each person I worked with on my team and worked for in management. The same holds true today in my roles as a team member or business consultant. I continue to educate myself by reading books and taking courses to enhance my own leadership skills.

If you see yourself leading your team inconsistently, step off the roller coaster and find a course or coach to teach you to more evenly manage the daily highs and lows of the workplace. Avoid taking it out on your team. You deserve less madness and so do those around you.

Chapter Takeaway:

CHAPTER 15 | IS YOUR SALES APPROACH OLDER THAN YOUR COMPUTER?

Work your way up or rust your way out

Successful sales professionals like to have the newest and latest technology. Whether the lightest and most feature-packed laptop or a smart phone that does everything but iron your shirts, salespeople are always looking for technology that can provide an edge over the competition. It's ironic these same people rely on sales calls and presentations that should have gone the way of the VCR and VHS tapes.

The average life span of a laptop is three to four years; I suggest you change your sales approach at least that often. Read books on business and sales or take workshops and seminars on those topics to learn new approaches. Otherwise, you'll operate as poorly and inefficiently as an old and slow computer.

Dinosaur Delivery

Times change and so do customers' expectations of salespeople. The days of the salesman being a sharply dressed smooth talker are over. The old sales thinking is, "I don't have a planned approach, and I just 'wing it'." You might believe that, but in reality you're just using the same old spiel, not adjusting to changing times and attitudes. (Note: it takes no effort to stay the same and get the same results.)

That old spiel focuses on your own agenda, not the prospect's. It might go something like this: Start with small talk, take a tour of the facility, talk about your company, roll out the brochure, talk about yourself, explain how bad the competition is, describe your company's capabilities, ask a few questions about the production volume or frequency, and end with a big closing question. Sound familiar?

The problem with this type of call is wasting valuable face time; you haven't spent a moment learning about the prospect's needs, goals and concerns. When you're with a prospective client, note how much of the time you spend talking, not listening. Most of that time is wasted. You can only learn something when you're asking questions and listening to the answers. There's no better way to have a conversation and build a relationship. Sure, people who do all the talking can still get business, but they'd get a lot more business a lot sooner if they'd just shut up already!

A More Modern Approach

Today's sales call isn't about you, the sales professional; it's all about the customer. You must know something about your customers—and your competition—before you arrive at their office and that takes homework. With the right preparation, prospects realize you're not wasting their valuable time by stumbling thoughtlessly through the meeting. Arriving prepared will make your approach more effective and professional.

Before you visit a prospective customer, go to the company's website and social media channels to learn as much as you can about the firm: its history and products, important news items, company events, and employees. Use that information to find similarities between that company and yours and create strategic questions to ask during your sales call.

Next, use the same approach to collect information about your competitors: their sales force, their strengths and weaknesses, their capabilities and services compared with your company's, and the "word on the street," or their reputation. Type that company's name into Facebook, Google or another search engine—you might find a discussion thread, a news story, or a research report that tells you more than the company's website. Note: It's worthwhile to search your company's name as well to learn about your online reputation.

In one of the workshops I offer on selling against the competition, participants dissect their top three (or more) competitors, identifying those companies' strengths and weaknesses and then developing strategies for selling against them. For example, if one of your competitors has reputation for great service, when you meet with prospective customers already using that company, your presentation should not mention service. To that customer, service is a given—they are already enjoying great service. Don't waste time talking about something they already have. When you know the competition, you can ask strategic questions rather than rote ones, questions you've created specifically to make people think.

Setting an Agenda

I repeat myself when stating how important it is to create an agenda for a sales call. You can follow the agenda to ensure that while you have face time, you are covering the points you identified during your research.

The agenda would include the questions you plan to ask—the ones that will allow you to collect the information you need to create a proposal and make a presentation that will result in a sale. Before I started using an agenda, I can't tell you how many times I walked out of a prospect's office without all the information I needed to make a presentation. Agendas keep the meeting on track. There's a reason why most meetings require them. As the result of a well-defined agenda you walk out with the information needed to take the next step in the process.

You can even share your agenda with the customer before the call. This differentiates you from your competition and shows your prospect that you have gone the extra mile to research the company and your competition and to ask targeted questions. Customers will be pleased to know they don't have to hear a canned presentation and endure another pushy sales call.

There is almost always one or two seasoned sales reps or leaders who are resistant to sales training as they do not want to be perceived as "not knowing." But those who attend with an open mind realize the information is invaluable. The combination of their own expertise and experience along with new formats is refreshing for them. It's the best of both worlds for the newbies who attend, and it will catapult them beyond their wildest expectations. So if your sales approach is older than your computer—or older than the advent of computers—be prepared to watch the others pass you by.

Chapter Takeaway:

CHAPTER 16 | FOR WOMEN ONLY

Professional myths and realities

News flash: If you are working in a male-dominated industry, it's no surprise you face some persistent negative stereotypes about your role and abilities. Unfortunately, some women's behavior reinforces those stereotypes. Don't rely on the fact that you're still a rare sight in a boardroom or industrial facility to make yourself stand out. Act professionally and people will focus on what you know and not on what you wear. Here are five myths about how women should act in a male-dominated workplace—and the realities I have learned in more than 30 years in the still male-dominated recycling industry.

Myth: Companies hire pretty girls to get the business.

Reality: Good looks do not make a successful salesperson—good sense does. Women in male-dominated industries are not wimps. Even the "lookers" must be knowledgeable and have good business sense. When they don't, they're here today and gone tomorrow. Industry knowledge, follow-through and professionalism are what achieve and sustain success.

Whether you work in a business office, conduct sales or operate heavy equipment, as a woman in a male-dominated industry, you must develop and follow a protocol that allows you to both be yourself and be part of a team. It is helpful to learn from a mentor who has experience in the industry.

Myth: If I jump on the crude-language bandwagon, it will help me be accepted.

Reality: Inappropriate language doesn't make you fit in, it just gives co-workers and customers the green light to send more your way. Before you know it, the language will cross the line into downright raunchy or even harassing.

Others might test you to see where you will draw the line and you should draw it right at the beginning. Most men would not want their mother, daughter, sister or wife to use inappropriate language while talking with them, so when you use foul language, you separate yourself from the women they most respect. If you can't help yourself, pick your moments—but never in a meeting, in anger, over a loudspeaker or chatting with a group of peers.

If you've already crossed that line with co-workers and customers, you can end it by simply abandoning that language. Others will quickly notice the change and follow suit.

Myth: Flirting is harmless.

Reality: Flirting with co-workers, prospects and customers might seem like fun, but it can lead to hurt feelings, ruined relationships or a damaged reputation.

What do I mean by flirting? I have been witness to many forms. Being overly attentive, giggling, sitting on a person's desk during a conversation, engaging in inappropriate physical contact, accepting inappropriate gifts, giving certain types of looks and taking too much interest in someone's personal life.

I know one male salesperson who flirted with a client over the phone and eventually set up a meeting with the intriguing voice at the other end. When they met, this salesperson was not physically attracted to the customer and was disappointed. I don't have to tell you what happened next. The person he rejected was the decision-maker and he lost the account.

When you're conducting business or simply with colleagues or customers— remain professional.

Myth: What I wear doesn't make a difference.

Reality: What you wear makes a big difference in how people treat you. If you think an outfit makes you look sexy, don't wear it in a professional situation, even if it's a social event. There is no business event where a revealing party dress with high heels and flashy jewelry is appropriate. Exposing cleavage or wearing tight, short clothing gives you zero credibility and makes you subject to ridicule.

While it may be fun to wear the latest fashions, take heed of your industry. Fashionable clothing works in some industries and not in others. What is professional in one industry can be unprofessional or unsafe in another. Taking a tour of a warehouse or manufacturing facility in stiletto heels or in a top with flowing sleeves isn't sensible and could result in injury. If you are in a conservative industry, dress sensibly and conservatively. No matter what your industry, seek guidance to the right choice of style. Save the fun stuff for your social life. You want to be taken seriously in the workplace.

Image consultants, business magazines and the internet are full of suggestions on what to wear for various business functions. Use them as a resource if you are unsure or think I don't know what I'm talking about.

Myth: Women should not be too aggressive in the business world.

Reality: There is a difference between aggressive and assertive and in business there is room for both. Aggressive and assertive men come across as powerful. Most people in business respect both of these traits. Scads of books, seminars and articles give advice on how to become a powerful woman in business. In my career I've found the following strategies valuable for standing my ground:

- Don't hesitate to talk about your value system.
- To earn respect, be honest and honorable. People talk about liars, they don't respect them.
- When you have a great idea, put it in writing or deliver it with others present in the room to ensure that other people don't use it as their own.
- Before blurting out how something is going to affect you, listen and get the facts. Otherwise, people will consider you a selfish loose cannon.
- Talk softly and slowly to maintain power. Women who get frustrated and emotional lose their edge.
- Remember that passion is a strength; use it.
- Wait 24 hours before responding when something irritates you. Never just react in the moment. Sometimes no reaction is better than a negative one.

By the way, men create the myths, we establish the reality.

Chapter Takeaway:

CHAPTER 17 | MIND YOUR MANNERS

The importance of etiquette

It's that time of year again—the busy social and holiday season. Time to eat, drink, and be merry with your customers and prospects. It's best to approach those get-togethers with manners as polished as your shoes. Even though manners reportedly are instilled in us between the ages of 4 and 8, fear not—it's never too late to improve your social graces.

Planning Ahead

If you plan to meet someone at a restaurant, my first tip is to make a reservation. If you're inviting a large party, visit the restaurant the day before your meeting and speak with the manager. If available, request a round table to make it easier for everyone to clearly see and interact with each other.

On the day of your meeting, be sure to arrive at the restaurant well before your guests. When you arrive early, don't be seated. It's polite to wait for your guests in the lobby and be seated together with them. Before your guests arrive, you can give the maître d' or server your credit card with instructions to automatically process the check at the end of the meal, including a 20 percent tip. Taking care of the check in advance prevents any uncomfortable moments for your guests. Yes, there are still men in the business world who feel uncomfortable when a woman pays. There are also people who never want you to pay, no matter what. This approach takes care of those situations. At the end of the meal, your guest may ask for the check, but you can reply, "It's all taken care of."

If you absolutely can't avoid being late, call the restaurant and explain your situation to the maître d'. Describe the members of your party (if you know what they look like) and ask the maître d' to inform your guests that you're running late and your expected arrival time. Ask the restaurant to seat your guests and offer them a beverage. Make sure you call as early as possible before your meeting time in case your guests are early. You are late when you realize you will be late, not at the time you are supposed to arrive.

Thanks ... a lot

Now let's talk about gratitude. Gratitude means being thankful. When someone brings me a drink and a meal I don't have to prepare or serve, I'm thankful. Any time anyone does anything for you in a restaurant—such as giving you an extra fork, taking away a used plate or delivering your drink, salad, entrée or dessert—say "thank you."

When a server asks what you'd like to drink, "Give me a Coke" is not a polite request; it's a command. When a server asks what type of dressing you'd like on your salad, "Thousand Island" is the wrong answer because "please" did not precede your reply. Instead, you can say, "I'll have a Coke, please" or "I'd like Thousand Island, please." See, that wasn't so hard! And when the server writes down your order and starts to walk away, it's a nice touch to add another "thank you."

Some might argue it isn't necessary to thank servers for everything or that the tip is the real thank you. Baloney. Whenever someone does something for you, just say thank you. The people serving you are individuals who like to be treated respectfully and appreciated for their work—same as you. The 'thank you' rule is universal and should be applied everywhere—at home, in the office, at a restaurant—and to everyone.

At the Table

Most people think their guests should order first and that is perfectly appropriate in many dining situations. That said, some guests may not feel comfortable ordering what they really want—like that 32-ounce T-bone steak—until you order or at least discuss what menu items interest you. So it's OK to order first and set your guests at ease. You can always change your order at the end.

The same holds true for dessert. Order it, even if you don't eat it. Your guests will follow your lead, especially if it's your first meal together. If you don't drink and your guests do, make sure they feel comfortable having a drink. If your guests don't drink, you have two choices—don't drink at all or drink moderately, such as a glass of wine or one beer. Do I hear moaning out there? Don't worry; you can survive one meal without your normal alcohol consumption. I speak from experience.

If you really want to shine, it's a nice touch to stand when your guests leave the table and when they return. Also, if someone approaches your table—such as a colleague, an acquaintance or a tardy member of your party—always stand up. I was once at a lunch with two brothers who owned a metal stamping business. When I excused myself to use the restroom, they both stood up. I was creeped out and thought they were coming with me. Then it dawned on me—only because I had seen that gesture once in a movie—that they were just being extremely polite. It made me feel special. Why not do that for someone? It's so easy. The exception is when you're seated against a wall and it would be difficult to stand, but that's a rare circumstance. Regrettably, you won't see much of this standing up stuff from folks in my generation or younger. It's a great way, though, to take your manners to a whole new level.

When leaving the table, place your napkin either on the seat or the back of your chair. Don't leave it anywhere on the table, and refrain from blowing your nose or wiping your forehead with your napkin throughout the meal.

If the table is full of plates, glasses and utensils, how do you know which is your stuff? The rule is: Liquids on the right, solids on the left. So that means your water glass is on the right; your bread plate is on the left. You use your utensils from the outside in. Of course, if someone at the table claims the wrong item, don't announce it, just go with the flow. Once again, remember that guests will follow your lead.

Here are some other points to consider when entertaining in public.

• Dress appropriately for the occasion.
• Don't raise your hand when trying to get the server's attention; try eye contact. The old joke about snapping your fingers and calling out "garçon!" is just that—a joke.
• Write notes to your guests after your meeting expressing how much you enjoyed getting together.

This advice is just the tip of the manners iceberg. Most people don't like to think they need a class on etiquette and manners, but there are simple rules that people just don't know. Even good people can have bad manners. Why not differentiate yourself from the competition by being courteous and well mannered? We polish our cars, our furniture and our nails—why not polish our behavior?

Chapter Takeaway:

CHAPTER 18 | ANY TIME IS A GOOD TIME TO SELL

Sales excuses are a dime a dozen

In 2009, what began as an economy of ups and downs turned into one of just downs and many companies found themselves in the red. It's not the first time the market has spiraled downward, but this time the global economy tanked. Consumers were not buying so manufacturers were not producing, which means they didn't need raw materials from their suppliers, and so on. An economy going nowhere means no receivables and no receivables means no payments to companies, vendors, and so on. As tough as the economic conditions were, it didn't mean all was lost. Even with a darkened financial forecast, I believe the best time to sell is always now.

When things are tough, it provides an opportunity for the sales professional to shine. Talented salespeople obviously enjoy the ride of good times in business, but they also know how to endure the tough times. If you lose customers now, it could mean they are struggling and trying to survive themselves, or it could mean they constantly shop the market looking for the best deal—and they've found something better than what you're offering. If that's the case, it's likely they were your customers for the wrong reasons. How do we meet the challenges of troubled times and make sure our customers are with us for the right reasons—regardless of the financial weather forecast?

Relationship Reminders

Communicate with your clients and prospects. That could mean monthly, weekly or daily—you need to know your customer's communication preferences. Make informational calls about what is happening in the industry. Send them links to relevant articles. Share with them what other companies are doing to weather the financial storm. Focus more time on building your relationship and less time on making the sale. Some of the best accounts are developed after the customer relationship is established.

Alternatively, be wary of prospects sniffing out pricing. Don't be too quick to respond to prospects who in the bad times, now want to talk. That's the equivalent of getting a call on Saturday morning for a date that night. It never really turns out well. If you do respond, just keep in mind that when things turn around, so might they.

Building Networking Muscle

Work on strengthening your formal and informal networking skills and opportunities. You never know where your next sale might come from. A good way to build your database of prospective customers is by asking your current customers for leads. Keep your eyes open for other networking opportunities, which could come in the form of trade shows or association meetings. Make sure you prepare for the event—just showing up isn't good enough. Know with whom you want to speak and what you want to say. Set clear goals and objectives. Ask open-ended questions when you meet people. Learn more about them and only take a few moments to tell them the essentials about you.

Confidence Counts

During difficult times, staying positive might be one of the more challenging things to do, but it's truly important. Staying positive and confident goes a long way toward building the customer's confidence in you. Along the same lines, keep in mind that you do not make yourself look good by making someone else look bad. Honesty and integrity should never take a back seat to anything. Take your integrity a step further by disputing any false rumors you might hear about your competitors. Such an act will go a long way toward showing others that you are an honorable person—someone with whom they want to do business.

Continue to build relationships with your current and prospective customers. The time will be well spent. Most important, keep your chin up. The economy is cyclical and we will all survive. This cycle will pass and when it does, you will find yourself on the other side of the economic fence with customers who value your commitment and prospects who might be ready for a change...

(This column was written in early 2009 during a global economic downturn and remember, history repeats itself.)

Chapter Takeaway:

CHAPTER 19 | THE VALUE OF FREE

Don't throw the baby out with the bathwater

I once took a trip that combined business and family time with my Uncle Bernie. I'm lucky to have an uncle like Bernie; just the thought of him makes me smile.

After calling on a prospect for nearly two years, I finally got my foot in the door with an opportunity to make a presentation to the sales team. The prospect was a five-star golf and tennis resort in northern Florida. The sales team's primary goal was to attract conferences and other groups to the property for a week of business meetings, banquets and golf outings. My goal for the visit was to provide a free sample of my training services. In exchange, the resort agreed to recommend me to customers who need a speaker or conference presenter with my expertise. It all seemed logical and worth the investment. After all, you have to spend money to make money, right? Sometimes, as I found out, you end up just spending money, but I learned a valuable lesson about the value of free.

A Change of Plans

My uncle, who lives in South Florida, proposed that I fly down to him—yep, fly right over my actual destination—and drive with him up to the resort. I agreed without hesitation and the road trip was on. There's nothing like a six-hour car trip for reconnecting and exploring, and there's no funnier travel companion than my Uncle Bernie.

Upon arriving at the resort, I began preparing for my presentation. I met the meeting planner for lunch and reviewed the list of workshop attendees and other details. Things were looking good. Then the phone rang. The resort asked if I had any flexibility on the presentation time. Of course I did so we rescheduled for a time later that day. Then the phone rang again. The presentation was canceled. The resort had reorganized that morning, terminating half of its sales team, and leadership thought it would be inappropriate for the remaining sales team to sit through a training program under the abrupt circumstances. As a businessperson, I understood; as a salesperson, I ached with disappointment and regretted the lost opportunity.

After regaining my composure, I poured myself a glass of wine and pondered what I could have done differently to ensure I met my goal even with the changed circumstances. In an effort to make me laugh, Uncle Bernie asked me to deliver my presentation for just him. I didn't laugh, but I did smile at the thought of him listening to my interactive workshop as an audience of one.

Learning the Lesson

My first mistake, I decided, was offering my workshop for free. Call it a habit from my days in the scrap industry. In scrap, we offer both inside and outside equipment for free. We offered customers free nonmetal recycling services in an effort to be more competitive. We didn't charge customers for our freight. The problem is, the customer doesn't comprehend or appreciate the value of a benefit it has never paid for. I had to ask myself, "What is the value of free? What is the value of our goodwill?"

You might think customers would value something free more when everyone is tightening their belts, but it's actually the opposite. Mostly, it's all about price. Customers focus on paying the least, regardless of what free services you've provided in the past. It's the "What have you done for me lately" approach. The harsh truth is that our customers are spoiled. Not only do we offer them a competitive price, but we also feel compelled to offer additional services just to keep on their good side. That approach isn't business as usual in other industries. When you buy a roast at the butcher, he doesn't give you a pan in which to cook it. When you purchase a computer or appliance, what additional free services do you get?

Here's a perfect example of my point: I managed a document destruction company for a client. On Saturdays, we would eagerly offer our mobile secure-shredding truck to banks so they could shred their customers' documents. We offered this service for free because we were looking for PR opportunities and to contract the banks up for the regular paid service. We found that the banks jumped at the free document destruction service but didn't advertise it to their customers, so no one showed up. I take that back—one time we shredded a shopping bag of confidential documents for an old lady who lived across the alley and heard our truck from her kitchen window. Once we started charging for the service, the banks had some skin in the game and a stake in the event's success, so they promoted it. The result? Lines of cars waiting to take advantage of the free service.

Though I wised up and stopped giving away our document destruction services, I fell into the "free" trap again with my training business, which the canceled Florida workshop made painfully clear. The lesson—all of us need to examine what we offer for free and why. More important, keep good records of what we do for free and remind our customers annually of those additional services—and what they save thanks to those perks.

In hindsight, I don't consider my Florida trip a bust. After all, I did get a road trip with Uncle Bernie, and I learned the value of free. It's time for you to do the same and then never waver.

Chapter Takeaway:

CHAPTER 20 | TEAMING UP FOR SUCCESS

Why two is better than one

As we waited for the economy to recover a few years back, companies on the brink of bankruptcy continued to merge with other firms in an effort to combine forces and survive the bad times. Businesses were reorganizing and examining their salespeople—assessing which ones delivered and which ones were resting on their laurels.

News flash: The old laurels have lost their value. You can sit in the sand and watch the surf or you can pick yourself up, grab your longboard, and get ready for the next wave. I recommend focusing on two essentials: hard work and teamwork. The salespeople who are serious about their jobs and the most valuable are the ones doing their best every day, bringing ideas to the table, and knowing how to be good team players. There's no longer a place for the salesperson who flies solo.

When a salesperson is allowed to handle accounts individually, that person often becomes an "account hoarder." Perhaps the person finds job security in being the only contact, or maybe he or she likes being a martyr ("Woe is me, my customers call me in the middle of the night and no one can help them but me"). If you have a hoarder on your sales team, know this: the situation can end in disaster. Sales department leadership should make it a point to know all their customers. One of my clients lost two of their largest customers when the solo salesperson for the accounts left the company. My client didn't even have contact names in the customer database, which made it difficult to save the accounts. The lesson: Companies must have the contact information for a minimum of 2 people in the customer organization. Visit your customers and get to know their key contact people, especially in the A and B type accounts. That information will enable you to step in promptly when there are changes—like when your solo salesperson seeks greener pastures. Had my client followed this advice, it might have been able to retain the customers in question.

The Team Approach

Better than the solo approach is having your salespeople obtain and maintain accounts jointly. Two or more talented people working together can create layers of relationships with prospects and customers, providing the impeccable service and constant communication that customers expect and appreciate. That effort can bring new business and increase account retention.

Team sales can be approached in a variety of ways. One common approach is to provide your accounts with other contacts at your company. The salesperson is not enough. Introduce your customers to accounting, logistics and other key roles in your organization. Another way is for two salespeople who work well together to form a team with one serving as the primary account manager and the other providing backup. In this arrangement, you could pair a hunter (skilled at landing accounts) with a farmer (talented at nurturing accounts) and create a synergy that allows each to do what they do best.

Some companies divide their sales force into teams, with a leader and team members working on the same territory. A team aligned to industry segments is another option. An example might be the salesperson, an account manager, customer service, and someone from accounting. This covers layers of strategic alliances.

Of course, some salespeople have never worked as team players and would find it difficult working that way. I know many narcissists who focus only on self-recognition and find it difficult to assist anyone else. Sometimes these people selfishly grab focus from others to make themselves appear more successful. Often the company culture breeds that behavior. When individual recognition and reward are the highest priorities, teamwork fails.

The Rules of the Sales Tag Team

There are rules to follow when working as a tag team and clear communication is the first and most important requirement. A shared calendar or client relationship management system (CRM) can keep the lines of communication open and inform all team members what is happening with each account. Respect and trust are other essential elements, and the three are related. If communication is lacking or inconsistent, the trust and respect in the relationship can potentially go south, as in any relationship. It's critical to communicate!

I once joined forces with a fellow salesperson and it couldn't have worked out better. Each of our accounts became accustomed to seeing us together and felt comfortable calling either of us to answer their questions and fulfill their requests. However, each account had a primary contact—the one who landed the account—and neither of us overstepped our boundaries. This team arrangement made each of us feel confident, knowing there was always abackup contact for our customers. And the customers had an added level of confidence knowing there were two high-level salespeople handling their business. The team approach also served our company by avoiding the curse of the solo salesperson. When I left to start my own consulting company, the accounts were informed and prepared and my departure was seamless.

Two Is Better Than One on a Sales Call

The team approach offers a lot of advantages. Having more than one salesperson at appointments, for example, gives your company more than one chance to connect. I invited a sales trainee on a sales call and watched her establish an immediate connection with the prospect based on his screensaver photo of a motorcycle. Unbeknownst to me, she was a biker. Their mutual passion for motorcycles made it easy to forge a relationship based on their shared interest and she closed the sale at our first meeting. That day I learned to sit back and enjoy the camaraderie that naturally developed. I also saw how passionate bikers are about their hobby. I was tempted to leave the appointment and head for the nearest tattoo parlor in celebration!

Whether your company can survive a recession intact or survive by merging with another firm, the smart salespeople are those who know how to work successfully with others. Become the best team player you can be. When your co-worker is in perfect position, find a way to help him or her score. Focus on the big picture and the success of your company, not just yourself. There are plenty of ways to win a game—and just as many ways to lose one. When using teamwork, the wins will surpass the losses and everyone benefits, but especially the customer.

Chapter Takeaway:

CHAPTER 21 | SUCCESS MEANS THINKING LIKE AN OWNER

How taking initiative will establish you as a leader

Often the best way to conduct business is by stepping into the shoes of another—especially if those shoes belong to the leaders of your company. Looking at the business from their point of view can help you see what your company needs to become stronger. The view from the top can positively affect the bottom line as well as strengthen your standing in the company.

I calculate the cost of every business move I make—whether it's for my company or someone else's—because I know what it feels like to take the risk and fear the fall. As a business person, you can do the same thing. Learn to make decisions as if you were the owner. That means weighing the costs and benefits of everything you do, treating each transaction as if your company's future depends on it, using time and resources wisely, and always asking yourself how else you can advance the company—even in ways beyond your job description.

Get Out and Sell

Whether I am selling my business or a client's product or service, I treat the sale as if the success of the company depends on it—because it does.

As a salesperson, you must do the same. Sell as if you are keeping the roof over your company's head. After all, that's what the company leaders do every day for you. They provide their teams with the financial means to take care of their families; now it's time for us to return the gesture. Think about what not having an income would mean to you and your family. You could become delinquent on your bills and fall deeper into debt with each passing month. Now apply that same way of thinking to your workplace. Stop making excuses about why it's not a good time to sell. Don't wait until the economy is better, imports/exports open up, the election is over, or summer ends. Just get out there and sell: make the calls and schedule the visits.

Save by Planning

Acquiring more business and generating a greater sales volume is just one piece of the puzzle. The smart use of resources is like an employee handing his or her employer a paycheck in return. Smart spending means taking a closer look at what you're doing now and asking yourself if you could do it better. Businesses—just like people—can get chubby, and shedding those extra resources often requires reflection and planning.

Start by better managing your time. One of the most annoying issues for leadership is disorganization, i.e. the team who arrives a few minutes late and then takes the first half hour of the day figuring out their schedule. Plan your week in advance. Know what you're going to do before you get to the office. That saves hours of time and translates into dollars. A variety of software applications can help you plan sales visits. In addition to saving time, you'll end up saving fuel and wear and tear on your vehicle. Obviously, there are always exceptions to the rule. If a huge sales opportunity comes your way don't worry about the mileage!

Restructuring your days can make you more efficient and allow you to do more in less time. But remember, leadership works a lot longer than 40 hours per week. Make sure your time is used wisely. In most cases, when logging your time, an hour can be gained by doing the right things at the right times. Use the "meat of the day" to increase sales and the rest to respond to emails and paperwork.

Lower-Cost Alternatives

In addition to wisely using your time, look for ways to save money. While I was discussing this column with a business associate, she summed up this point quite nicely: "People need to ask, would I create this expense if it were my money?"

If your company entertains its customers, find less expensive venues. For example, minor-league sports teams are a good alternative to the major leagues. The action comes with a much smaller price tag and the teams show their appreciation by providing pure entertainment from beginning to end. The concessions and parking cost less, too. Plan an event for your customers' children or grandchildren. If you haven't done that before, you're in for a pleasant surprise and it's a great way to strengthen your relationship with your customer.

If you prefer dining with your customers, why not invite them to your home for a casual barbeque? My guess is that you will never lose a customer who has enjoyed an evening at your home. If the idea of home entertaining makes you queasy or sends your spouse to a divorce attorney, try finding a more affordable dining venue. Upscale and well-known steakhouses aren't necessary. Neighborhood joints often serve better food, provide a more intimate setting, and—like the minor-league teams—care that you're there. They depend on you.

Pitch In Wherever You Can

And lastly, ask yourself, "How else can I serve my company?" Owners often wear more than one hat. Think about what other skills you can share with your employer. If, in addition to being a sales pro, you have superior computer, marketing, operational or leadership skills—share them. Bring new ideas to the table and assist in streamlining processes and procedures.

Offer a helping hand to those who can't keep up. No matter where I have worked, I make it a point to ask if I can do more. I bring in new ideas and processes that have demonstrated value and then we implement them. While working with a client in the area of employee development, I asked if I could be involved in their document shredding subsidiary. It gave me an opportunity to learn a new business, and they leveraged my strengths in sales, operations and leadership to grow their new division. It all happened because I made a suggestion.

By thinking as your company's owner, you help your company and yourself. It's important to think outside the box, much like the entrepreneurs who employ you—and me. Keep the roof over the employers' heads, and they will keep the roof over yours.

Chapter Takeaway:

CHAPTER 22 | EFFORT AND ACHIEVEMENT

Defining the role you play on your team

One Sunday last summer, I tried to rally my family for church. Attending church as a family during the summer is a challenge for my loved ones because it means they have to choose between sitting in a pew for an hour or more instead of playing golf or sleeping. On this particular day, I lost the battle and drove to church alone. I arrived late, so I slipped quietly into the second-to-last row.

My church reserves the last row for adult congregants with physical and mental disabilities, many of them in wheelchairs. During the opening hymn, I heard the folks behind me trying their best to sing or hum along. I glanced back and saw the joy on their faces. Just after the hymn, the minister invited all of us to greet our neighbors. I turned, exchanged morning salutations, and shook their hands. The physical and mental abilities of the last-row worshippers might be different from the other worshippers, yet there they were, seated in their reserved row, on time and happy to be there (unlike my family). That moment inspired me to think about effort.

Effort is often associated with words such as strenuous, earnest, hard work and achievement. Almost everything in life—including your reading this sentence—requires effort. Many of us remember report cards with a teacher's note stating: "Johnny is a good student but doesn't apply himself." In a review, leadership might encourage a worker to use his or her initiative and creativity—to put forth more effort—to achieve better results. Effort, in short, is the foundation of success.

Bee Basics

People point to the insect world for examples of effort leading to success, whether it's the fable of the industrious ant and the lazy grasshopper, or the efficiency and productivity of bees. In my sales training career, I've noticed that companies are very much like bee colonies, with the sales team functioning as the bees: They move constantly to achieve their sales goals, and once they achieve one, they move tirelessly on to the next target. Each effort is an important step toward achieving the ultimate goal of the company's success (or, for a bee, the colony).

I've observed that just as there are several types of bees in each colony, there are three basic types of team members in a company, each delivering effort in his or her own way. First you have the queen bee. So I don't sound sexist, I'll call this the sales/entrepreneurial bee. This bee is the most vital individual in the colony. The sales/entrepreneurial bee supplies the rest of the colony with accounts and vision to keep the colony in the black. This bee, however, does not die after delivering its first sting (landing its first account). The sales bee continually applies the effort needed to build the colony.

Next are the worker bees. They follow up dutifully on leads passed their way, work hard to develop and maintain strong relationships, and have a solid understanding of all aspects of the business, such as accounting and operations. Unfortunately, they get caught up in the colony's busy work and often lack focus on their individual results. Though they are responsible individuals who devote great effort to their jobs, they seldom see the rewards in their paychecks and spend most of their time protecting the health and well-being of the other bees in the colony.

Then there are the drones, the most disposable bees in the colony. The worker bees feed them until they are no longer needed. If the drones would just boost their efforts, they could become worker bees, but they don't feel it's worth the energy.

The worshippers in the back row of my church exhibited effort on par with a queen bee. My guess is that they woke up earlier that Sunday morning than most other congregants because it takes them more time and effort to get ready and make the long haul to church. They didn't moan or groan about attending (like my family), but instead they sang songs of praise as loud as their lungs would allow. Like the queen bee, they were the most vital people in the church that day, inspiring me. I know in my heart they will deliver that same effort, week in and week out. And because of what I learned from them, so will I.

Chapter Takeaway:

CHAPTER 23 | THE CASE FOR TRAINING

Turning ordinary salespeople into extraordinary contributors

Henry Ford reportedly once said, "Anyone who stops learning is old, whether at 20 or 80." He was emphasizing the importance of continuous learning. In my work as a sales trainer, however, I run across a lot of people—especially veteran salespeople—who resist learning. Regardless of your age or the stage of your career, I think you should take advantage of every learning opportunity. Learning is how we arrived at where we are today and how we'll get to where we'll be tomorrow.

Setting a Good Example

When doing training work for companies' sales, leadership and customer-service associates, I'm delighted when the leaders who hire me are excited about giving their teams the opportunity to expand their education and expertise. They want to be involved; they help me customize the training for their crew; and they attend the training themselves, knowing that they will learn something valuable as well. Their presence sets a great example for their teams and clearly shows how they value the importance of training. To quote Albert Schweitzer, "Setting an example is not the main means of influencing others, it is the only means." Their participation also enables them to better assist with implementing the training after I have gone, which otherwise could become a challenge.

In contrast, I've dealt with plenty of company leaders who floated in and out of the training session or sat in the room answering emails and texts, taking important calls or looking at their watches. Aside from being irritating as hell, such behavior sends the wrong message to the other participants. If your behavior suggests that the training is not important, then your team won't perceive it as important either. It is better if they excuse themselves rather than be disruptive.

Old Dogs, New Tricks

Some clients hire me to train their new teams. Though I like teaching neophytes, I can't help but feel sorry for the veteran salespeople who have never received opportunities for professional development in their entire careers. Instead, many of them relied on what worked when they started their sales jobs. Most of the time it's the "Get out the old brochure and review the bullet points" or the "I tell, they listen" sales approach. News flash: Times have changed and old sales methods don't work anymore. Older salespeople can't—or shouldn't—rely on their positions of authority or seniority simply to maintain the status quo. I've trained young salespeople who could run circles around the people who are supposedly leading them. If you keep learning, you avoid becoming a dinosaur and will be more in sync with your sales team, young and old, which will make the whole group more unified, professional and successful.

Some companies offer training but make it optional. I believe training should be required. Based on my experience, young salespeople can't wait to take it all in while most veterans opt out. The vets feel they don't need the training or don't want others to perceive them as weak or "uninformed." Some veterans attend for kicks and usually disrupt the sessions. They talk loudly to their friends from the back row and wander out. When they return after an hour of missed information, they join the discussion and preach their old methodology. Some haven't made a cold call or sales call for years. In general, the longer a salesperson is around, the more he or she can depend on referrals, which are a whole different type of call. That's why they think the old methods still work.

What they don't realize is that they haven't kept up with the times. Today's customers and prospects are more sophisticated, and they want to be heard, not talked at. If you make it to their respective conference rooms, chances are they know all about your company, have visited your firm's website, and reviewed research from the Better Business Bureau, Dun & Bradstreet, LinkedIn, Google, Twitter—and that's just the old folks. The young professionals are looking you up on Facebook, Instagram, YouTube and whatever else is the next big thing. They're meeting with you to determine if you can help them, and the only way you can do that is by asking open-ended questions that reveal their needs. Learning to ask the right questions is the key to shortening the sales cycle. Before walking in the door, it is important to know in great detail what your company can do to assist the prospective customer. If you go in unprepared, you'll look unprofessional and old.

Training "In the House"

Sometimes clients hire me to assist in organizing intracompany training. In these cases, a knowledgeable person on the team becomes a "trainer" by sharing his or her expertise with co-workers. When the person knows what he or she is doing, it can be a positive experience, promoting information sharing across departments and expanding the knowledge of all participants. In many instances, unfortunately, the in-house trainers don't know how to engage the audience or even create an interesting presentation. They just talk and talk. I can't help but think of the scene in Ferris Bueller's Day Off when the teacher poses a question, then asks, "Anybody? Anybody?" to a classroom of unengaged students who are ready to throw themselves off a bridge.

In one of the worst sessions I've ever witnessed, the industry expert turned trainer forced attendees to take a test about the chemistry of various metals. No one was made aware of the pop quiz. After grading the tests, the trainer called attendees to the front one by one, announcing their scores and humiliating people who had been in the industry for years. The person sitting next to me fittingly called it "The Walk of Shame."

The moral of the story is to take the time to review any and all content for workshops and seminars for both intracompany and outsourced training. Think about who will attend, and make sure they are open to a new approach. The time wasted rehashing old methodology is expensive and unproductive. Also—though this may sound like a no-brainer—people who attend training sessions should emerge invigorated and uplifted by the experience, not humiliated. Professional instructors know the ropes so if you use personnel from inside your ranks for training, simply look at their agenda before the training. Finally, talk with the attendees after the training. Ask them what they considered helpful and what they plan to apply in their careers. When done right, training is what turns ordinary salespeople into extraordinary contributors.

Chapter Takeaway:

_____

_____

_____

CHAPTER 24 | WHY I HATE THIRD PARTY ADMINISTRATORS

When the goal of efficiency becomes inefficient

We all have things we hate at one time or another in life. As a kid, maybe you hated adults who pinched your cheeks, doing homework, attending any type of school in the summer, eating liver and onions for dinner, or enduring parents who told stories about you to their friends. During adolescence most of us hated discipline, people who held us accountable, and any advice from our parents. When we became adults, I'd like to think we left behind a lot of our hating habits. Yes, there are circumstances that continue to make us unhappy, but we learned that it isn't good to hate anything. We learned to get along and work around life's obstacles. It's called growing up. I'm proud to report that I had a long streak of hateless years. Everything was smooth sailing, and life was good. Then I received a request for quote (RFQ) from a buying group.

Some prospects—usually large companies—hire such groups to expedite requests for quotes (RFQs). These third-party administrators are bad news for the vendors who bid on the contract. The winning bidder not only has to almost eliminate profit with a low price, but it also must pay the buying group a monthly fee based on a percentage of the customer's expenditure. If the vendor charges $100,000 to the customer one month, it also would be contractually obligated to pay the buying group, say, 3 percent of that total, or $3,000. The vendor that gets the contract must pay that fee on time, or the buying group could increase the percentage. Also, the group states in the contract that the client must be paid according to a set formula in a certain number of days, or else the contract will be null and void. The buying group leaves no room for unexpected developments, such as a financial tsunami or even a real tsunami.

If your company wins one of these contracts, you may feel—initially—that you landed a windfall, but the truth is that most of these deals give the vendor little leeway to turn a profit. The customer teams up with the buying group to take the wind out of the vendor's sail. Then they take the sail and sell it on eBay or Craigslist, leaving the vendor lost at sea.

The RFQ Gauntlet

To explain why I dislike—OK, hate—these arrangements, let me walk you through my experience with an RFQ process. First I had to beg, borrow and steal just to get my client on the list of companies who could bid on the contract.

We waited for what seemed like months to receive an invitation to begin the process. We had to maneuver through a web portal that was not user-friendly and fill out a 43-page form. The confidential information the application required included company financial details, a list of current customers, my personal bank account number—you get the idea.

Shortly after we received the RFQ, the third-party administrator allowed us to visit only some of the prospects' locations, visits during which we got little to no helpful information to base the numbers for our quote. The administrator did not completely understand the scope of service and I found myself walking his representatives through the process—when I was allowed to speak with them. Their ignorance of the situation was clear in that the RFQ was designed more for purchasing widgets than for contracting a service. The administrator's corporate office was elusive, relying on its uninformed reps to do the job.

The RFQ itself took weeks to prepare; the entire process took seven months. It was not just my time, but the time of the accounting department and logistics team. During the process, I analyzed the competition and crunched numbers on both the service and the sale of the commodity dozens of times. I became the Queen of Spreadsheets.

Much like an auction, the process allowed no interaction with the customer. Unless you were the incumbent vendor, there was precious little information on which to base your pricing. There was a place on the front of the bid for comments. I spent hours wordsmithing my comments to make sure they would draw in the bid reviewers. The comments were my only chance for some interaction or communication that was not in the form of a web-based questionnaire. I found out later in the process that no one even read the comments.

During this type of bid, ego begins to rear its ugly head and the buying group counts on that psychology. The more time competing bidders invest in the RFQ, the more committed they are to fight to win, and the more the buying group allows bidders to become even more aggressive in their quotes.

If the RFQ had been for widgets, it might have worked, but in this situation it was a disaster. We were quoting a service with value-added variables and we were proposing a program different from any other they had ever seen. We were offering recycling services that would save the company in waste disposal costs. The RFQ for waste was open for bid at the same time. You'd think it would be easy to look at both programs and see the synergies between them—how less of one could mean more of the other. Seeing the similarities would have helped the customer. No matter how much we tried to explain that logic to the buying group, its reps were unable to grasp the concept.

Thanks, But No Thanks

In the end, I did not win the bid. We weren't the only company to jump through hoops at great expense to find out that the incumbent vendor won the job.

When I received the "thanks, but no thanks" email from the buying group, it was like being fired on a Post-it Note. My guess is that the third-party administrator sought to use the bidders to drive the incumbent's price to an all-time low while not having to make any changes. No transition, no learning curve, just a rock-bottom fee from the vendor—and, of course, their own fees from the prospect and the winning vendor.

Though buying groups might work in certain circumstances, in this particular case the group did a disservice to its customer. It ignored synergies that could have improved the customer's operations and saved it money. Where is the benefit in that? I imagine this contract will be up for bid again in a couple of years, and I will receive a new RFQ. My reply will be "thanks, but no thanks" on a Post-it.

Chapter Takeaway:

CHAPTER 25 | PLANNING A SUCCESSFUL TEAM SALES CALL

Avoiding a shit show

A team sales call, as you might guess, is when two or more sales reps from a company call on a prospect or customer. Though some old-timers in sales (you know who you are!) consider it a waste of time to have two or more high-level salespeople on one call, I politely disagree. To me, it makes perfect sense. When you're meeting with a team, you should bring your own team. You wouldn't go into battle alone, unless you're Iron Man. Far from being a sign of weakness, a joint sales call is an effective sales approach that those with confidence and high self-esteem should welcome. If you've never brought another person on an important call, I advise you to rethink your sales game plan.

The Right Approach

There's a right way and a wrong way to do joint sales calls. If your team doesn't take the right approach and executes such calls poorly, your company will look lackluster and unprofessional. Believe me, I've seen the good, the bad, and the downright embarrassing in my years as a sales professional. On the good side, I used to work with a company in the metals industry that had an all-male sales team that demonstrated exemplary teamwork skills. (I'm happy to report that the company has hired some female salespeople since then.) I knew many of the salesmen and admired their approach. When dealing with prospects and customers, they projected the image of being a closely-knit fraternity, and they made most of their contacts want to join their ranks.

What made this team stand out? Among other attributes, the team members dressed professionally, each wearing a tie every day. They went through extensive etiquette training and behaved accordingly. When they spent time with prospects and customers, they came across as a cohesive group, all on the same page. Most important, they didn't compete with each other in front of prospects or customers; instead, they worked together with one goal in mind—to provide solutions and good service to their clients.

More recently, I worked with a sales colleague who is a pro at the joint call. We played off each other well, which makes prospects and customers feel at ease because more than one individual is working their account. We went in with the same goal: to succeed for our employer. When taking this account to lunch one summer, they asked me why I didn't bring my "sidekick." They were used to spending time with both of us.

Follow the Rules

To execute a successful joint sales call, you only need to follow some basic rules, many of which you learned in kindergarten.

Be nice to and respect each other. If you want a functional, rather than a dysfunctional, sales team, you must be nice to each other. There's no place for sour grapes and baggage when preparing for or participating in a sales call.

It essentially comes down to respect. If you go on a call feeling superior to a teammate, or you're disrespectful to someone on the team, it will be crystal clear to the prospect or customer. Think about those times you've been around spouses who aren't getting along. It's downright uncomfortable, isn't it? Unless you like watching train wrecks, all you want to do is bolt. That's exactly what your prospect or customer will feel if the members of your sales team show disrespect or are out of sync with each other.

Play well together and share. Sales, like life, is a process of give and take. When a sales team makes a call and one member has his or her own agenda, it's a turnoff to the prospective customer. If a member of your sales team hogs the spotlight, speaks more than the others, pulls out an unexpected presentation or interrupts, it exudes unprofessionalism. Leave your ego at the door to be a positive, contributing member of a sales team. No individual salesperson should dominate a joint sales call.

Sharing starts long before the sales call and it carries beyond the call to the follow-up, and then into the ongoing service and relationship of the account. The team members must share information both before and after the call to truly succeed. Also, be a good listener. Take a lesson from the children's poem about the wise old owl, which teaches that you learn more when you listen than when you speak.

Don't be a tattletale. I've heard salespeople go on a joint call and then return to the office and complain about their team members. If you are leading the team, this is a huge red flag. Don't let this happen. Support the salesperson who comes back enthusiastic and thinking about the good in the call, not the one who is worried about who gets credit. My mother told me when I was 9 years old, "You don't make yourself look good by making your brother look bad." That was the last time I tattled.

Develop a Plan That Works

Joint sales calls are no different than solo calls in that they require advance preparation and thought. It is essential to meet beforehand to discuss the meeting's content, prepare an agenda and a list of open-ended questions, and perhaps create and practice the presentation, which can help the team stay on point during the call. The agenda and presentation can be especially helpful in meetings when a prospect or customer seems intent—intentionally or not—on taking the conversation off track. Armed with preparation and the right tools, your team members can remain focused, support each other, and achieve the desired sales goals.

At times, it might make sense for your team to include not only your salespeople but others in your company with knowledge in specific areas like accounting or information technology. They could explain your company's billing or payment processes as well as its technological advantages. If certifications are a hot button for the target company, bring your own compliance specialist to answer any questions. The team approach might seem strange to the salespeople who are used to flying solo, but remember that even Iron Man needs some backup from time to time. Cue Captain America.

Chapter Takeaway:

CHAPTER 26 | A WHINE CONNOISSEUR

Sales excuses are a dime a dozen part two

They are known by many names—grumbler, moaner, squawker, bellyacher, crybaby, kvetcher—and they are everywhere. They are salespeople with a gripe and they take up valuable time with their co-workers, leaders, friends, and relatives with their whining.

Why do some people need to provide an incessant drone of complaints? The reasons vary, but the underlying sentiment always is the same—they feel discontent over the current state of affairs. I confess, I have little patience for whiners. When I hear someone whine, I want to do what Cher did to Nicolas Cage in *Moonstruck*—slap the person in the face and say, "Snap out of it!" (Google it. It's funny.)

Pragmatic teams simply change direction if they don't like the way things are going. They don't need the leadership to chart their course or carry them over the hurdle. Just a few tweaks and they're back on track. These team members simply refuse to be whiners themselves or fall prey to others' complaining ways. If you're a chronic complainer, take this opportunity to change your tune. Here's a list of six common whines and how to turn destructive thoughts into constructive ones.

Whine No. 1: I don't have enough time. The hair on my arms stands up when I hear salespeople complain about not having enough time. Having enough time really is a matter of making enough time. By arriving an hour or so earlier a few days a week, for example, you can create the time you need. Take a half-hour lunch instead of an hour, and you gain two-and-a half hours a week. Or just be more efficient with your time. According to a Microsoft survey, teams say they are unproductive an average of 16 hours a week, so stop talking, smoking, reading internet jokes, and checking your social media accounts, and you'll find even more time.

If your time shortage stems from taking on more work than you can manage, ask yourself what you can do about it. Unless you're a superb time manager, think twice before volunteering to take on additional work. Yes, carrying a heavy work-load can be admirable, but it can be a death sentence for your career if you can't carry through on everything you've promised. It's much like writing a bad check. Insufficient time is the same as insufficient funds.

Whine No. 2: I don't get what I need from leadership. In difficult times, teams tolerate poor leadership due to the lack of other job options, and then they whine about it. Even in good times, though, this is a frequent cause for grumbling. After all, it's easy to blame someone else for problems and not take any accountability for them yourself.

These types of complaints usually fall into two categories, either not enough or too much oversight. Some team members desire more face time, better training and constant support and interaction from leadership. When new at the company, they need all of the above. If they find themselves still needing all of that after they've been around a while, then they should assess their ability to use their own initiative and start making some of their own decisions.

Conversely, if you're being micromanaged, it might be time to find a new position. Micromanagers seldom change without intervention. If you're the only one on the team being micromanaged, however, take that as a sign that your efforts aren't up to par and leadership feels the need to keep a close eye on you.

Whine No. 3: I don't have the right tools. There's an old saying that great meals are made in old pots. In other words, you don't need to have brand-spanking-new tools to get great results. I have little respect for salespeople who complain about not having the tools they need. I began my sales career with a business card and a brochure that was so unattractive I chose not to use it. With today's technology and social media options, there's no limit to what salespeople can create or have created for them. If your company doesn't have a newsletter, for instance, you can make your own and distribute it through social media to your customers and prospects. You can write a blog or contribute articles on LinkedIn. There are a ton of options if you use your initiative.

If you don't have the right technology, purchase it yourself and then show your company's leadership the benefits of the investment. Chances are your employer will see the advantages. If your company's brochure, website and social media aren't up to par, approach leadership with good ideas—and price quotes—to update the items. An overhaul of a website can be a significant undertaking, so finding a cost-effective way to accomplish it is essential.

Whine No. 4: We're under-teamed. Seems the new norm is for companies to do more work with fewer people. If you have this complaint, you're not alone. In my consulting work, I have yet to run across a single company that I'd consider over-teamed and I don't see the tight teaming situation changing anytime soon. What can you do about this situation? See Whine No. 1.

Whine No. 5: I'm underpaid. Complaining about compensation and benefits will get you some extremely negative attention. Whining that "I've worked here longer, but so-and-so makes more money" will get you nowhere. Larger companies have clear-cut compensation and benefits packages. You can walk over to HR and find out where you are in the range. If you don't like what you find, ask what you can do to change the situation.

The reality is that not all companies have opportunities for advancement for every position. Your options will vary depending on the nature of the company. Further, in less-sophisticated firms, salaries and bonuses can be arbitrary or based on how the year, month, day or moment is shaping up. It helps if you know the lay of the land in this regard before you accept a position. If you're already there, there's no harm in talking to the appropriate people about what opportunities you have for professional growth or a higher salary—just don't whine if you don't get the answer you want.

If you want to rise from sales to leadership and the company isn't structured for that type of progress, you can either wait around for someone to leave or die, or you can move on—it's your choice. Just don't stick around and complain. It isn't healthy for anyone, especially you.

Whine No. 6: Nobody appreciates me. My least favorite whine is when teams gripe that leadership isn't giving them the attention they deserve. My advice: Try doing something outstanding and you'll definitely get and keep your leader's attention.

Chapter Takeaway:

_____

_____

CHAPTER 27 | WATCH YOUR LANGUAGE, DUDE

Pitfalls of being too trendy when communicating

There are several languages spoken in the business world, but the language with which I'm most familiar—standard American business English—is heading for the endangered species list. The use of idioms, clichés and slang in business seems to be at an all-time high, and I think these communications shortcuts are impeding our ability to understand one another and "dummying down" some intelligent people.

Idioms—expressions with a figurative meaning that differs from their literal meaning (think "kick the bucket")—have most likely existed since the inception of communication and commerce. Somewhere on a cave wall, there's probably a drawing of "low-hanging fruit" the cave people used to symbolize some other easy-to-accomplish task. We all strive to "think outside the box." I have figuratively "pushed the envelope" and "hit the ground running." And I've worked at companies that "silo" their information and departments while trying to "stay on message" and "bring something to the table."

Though I've heard and used these terms throughout my career, I've had a "paradigm shift" in my feeling toward such language. In short, it's starting to irritate me.

Communicating—or Not

To understand the problem with such language, it helps to think about why we use it. Some people hear these terms and start using them without even realizing it. What's worrisome is when they didn't understand the term in the first place. Others use business idioms, jargon and clichés because they think it will make them sound informed and up on modern lingo. (They're wrong; they sound like followers.) Still other individuals and companies create their own buzzwords—earning themselves points for creativity. Regardless, I have little patience for this language anymore. It can impede communication—especially when communicating across generational or cultural lines—and the overused terms have become meaningless.

Want an example? A few years back, I attended a meeting with some young professionals at a large insurance company. They said hiring a company like mine had been on their "whiteboard." After discussing "initiatives" and "optimization," they decided their company would "partner" with my firm. I walked out grateful to have the business, but I was mentally exhausted. I ran to a bookstore and found a handbook of sorts—*A Dictionary of Bull****: A Lexicon of Corporate and Office-Speak* by Diane Law, and used it often. Unfortunately, it is now out of date and I need an updated version.

A new use for an old word also can confuse—or annoy. In the last year or so, I think I've heard the word "gotcha" about 200 times a day. People now use it to mean they understand what you're saying. Co-workers nod in meetings and say "gotcha." I explain a new sales technique to a trainee, who responds with "gotcha." When I was growing up, we said "gotcha" when we caught up with a person we were chasing. It is not a business word. It means "I captured you." Why can't we simply state that we understand? When I ask young professionals to refrain from saying "gotcha," they nod and say, "My bad."

Here's another example of slang replacing business courtesy: A few months ago, I invited a colleague to an event and she responded saying she would "take a pass" on it. I take it personally when someone takes a pass on anything I offer. I would have preferred she say, "Thanks for your thoughtful invitation, but I'm unable to attend." No explanation needed. For those of you who are "taking a pass" these days, you might want to find a less abrasive way to decline an invitation. Imagine your best customer giving you a call and saying that he or she is going to "take a pass" on working with you.

For many years, one of the most popular idioms was for someone to "touch base" with a colleague or customer, meaning he or she would contact that person. Today we no longer touch base, we "reach out." When people tell me that they will be "reaching out" to someone, I immediately think of a hand stretching out to grab someone who is drowning. Please don't reach out to me. Just call me back. That'll work.

And if business clichés and jargon were not annoying enough, language that might be OK among friends has crept into the business world. I've even heard my husband—who is very conservative—use the word "dude" in a business setting. Here's a news flash: Some people don't like being called "dude." Some people just aren't "dude" material. Also, an adult who uses the word "dude" does not sound like an adult.

Swearing Like a Business Professional

Idioms, clichés, jargon and slang are annoying and can impede communication, but swearing is something else entirely. Some work environments seem to accept swearing, which is something I just don't understand. I can't believe how many businesspeople are unable to complete a sentence without a swear word. They swear in meetings, while standing around having casual conversations with coworkers and loudly and obnoxiously on their end of a phone conversation. And sadly, they don't care who hears them or if anyone in earshot is offended. They are human resource time bombs.

At a formal event, I once talked with a 25-year-old male acquaintance whose every other word was some variation of the "F-bomb." I asked if he felt comfortable using that language with me. "Yes," he replied, suggesting to me that he simply has no language filter. An intern who worked for me one summer had a different theory: "One must know better before one can use a filter." To me, it's just plain old common sense: Swearing in a business setting is inappropriate and disrespectful.

Though I might not like business idioms, they can be entertaining—when they aren't rude—and they're here to stay. People just seem to love a good buzzword or phrase, even if it isn't the best communication vehicle. The good news is that if you master such idiom-speak, I'm pretty sure you can call yourself bilingual.

Chapter Takeaway:

CHAPTER 28 | DEVELOPING A TASTE FOR GOAL-SETTING

Tools for measuring achievement

"Success is not having the same problem a year later."

I love that quote and I try to live by it as it forces me to set goals that bring about change and forward movement in my life. Each time we begin a new year or a new job/position, it's the perfect time to review our accomplishments and our unreached goals, and then set some new ones.

Every year I set professional and personal goals. (It's important to set both to have some semblance of a balanced life—and, yes, I'm talking to all you workaholics out there.) Below are my work-related goals from last year, with notes about my progress on each and an overall achievement rating. (Keep in mind that I wrote this in mid-November, so I still had six weeks to get my act together on some of these.)

Keep current. I kept up with the news, but I could have read more, attended more cultural events, and so on. On the plus side, I studied generational leadership. Score: 75 percent.

Revamp website. Just finished another revamp (check it out at www.judyferraro. com). Score: 100 percent.

Create at least two new fun workshops or seminars. Developed "Communication in a Technology-Driven Environment" and "What Just Happened?" (Both contain only exercises and loads of fun, trust me). Score: 100 percent.

Help my clients grow their businesses. I sometimes get caught up in the day-to-day operations of my long-term clients, which causes me to lose focus on my sales strengths. Score: 80 percent.

Share business talents in the community. Involved on church leadership team. Score: 100 percent.

Write more interesting columns and blogs that provoke reader interaction. I received more feedback on my column last year than ever before. I love hearing from readers (hint, hint). Score: 100 percent.

My personal goals covered the gamut, from volunteering to exercise, wrapping up a book I'm writing, and to staying funny (which I believe I achieved 100 percent—what can I say?). In the interest of brevity, I won't enumerate them all here, but you get the picture.

So there you have it, the goal-setting and goal-reviewing process. Simple as that. At the end of the year, I shift the uncompleted items to short-term goals. I rewrite the old standbys and think of new ways to realize them. Then I add new goals for the year and review everything monthly.

Try It, You'll Like It

People who resist the goal-setting process remind me of live fish flopping around on the deck of a boat, trying to get back to the water. They know where they want to go but aren't exactly sure how to get there. They expend great energy in the fight but rarely achieve their goal. The same could be said of working and living without putting your goals down on paper. When you don't take the time to control your destiny and life, other people often will control it for you.

I've heard a lot of excuses for why people don't set goals. "I don't have to write down my goals because I know them in my head." "I've never written down my goals, and I've still managed to be successful." "I think that writing goals is stupid/corny/a waste of time." My answer is always the same: "You may have your goals in your head and be successful, but haven't you ever felt off track, unfocused or overwhelmed?" And the reply is always, "Yes." Goals are a map to keep you on track or help you get back on track if you're lost.

Writing down your goals and tracking your progress on them isn't a scary, unpalatable process. You could liken it to trying a certain food—you might think you dislike it, but once you give it a try, you find that it's quite good. That certainly was the case about eight years ago with one of my customers, a young executive who was far from eager to write goals. At my urging, he gave it a try and agreed to share his first round of goals here, complete with notes on how he planned to achieve each goal and his assessment of his progress.

Grow the business and profit margins. Hire at least one outside salesperson and one inside salesperson, and seek new methods to obtain business, such as advertising and networking. Result: Hired an outside salesperson and joined two industry-related organizations. Profit margins could be better. Score: 60 percent.

Hire key accounting and sales personnel. Hire a controller in accounting and (as noted above) both inside and outside sales reps. Result: Hired a controller and outside sales rep, but still need an inside salesperson. Score: 65 percent.

Help teams grow. Encourage every team to complete two training workshops or seminars that will enhance his or her career and personal life. Result: The operations team took one safety seminar. Score: 50 percent.

Work on safety in the company. Provide safety training and write safety procedures/ handbook. Result: Completed the training, but still working on the handbook. Score: 75 percent.

Speak at two events. Volunteer to speak at a local chamber of commerce meeting and other forums. Result: Never got around to it. Score: 0 percent.

This young executive also set personal goals, such as mentoring outside the workplace, reading more, and—one of my favorites—refraining from looking at his phone when people are talking to him (how many of you could achieve that goal?).

Though the above goals were not overly aggressive, they were a great start. What they taught this young executive was to be accountable to his business, his family and himself. Now, every year he jots down his goals. He even has called to make me aware of a midyear addendum to his list of goals. In addition to realizing some personal accomplishments from this practice, he has seen his business grow from $3 million in revenue to $8 million in five years. I can't take full credit for that growth, but I will take credit for an assist.

Chapter Takeaway:

_____

_____

_____

CHAPTER 29 | THE REWARDS OF RECOGNITION

The power of praise

Who doesn't like to be recognized for a job well done? That's what I thought. Everybody likes to be recognized. It's a universal human need, and it's just as important in our professional lives as it is in our personal lives. For most people, being recognized for doing something great begins when they're babies (perhaps with their first burp) and continues throughout their lives—when they take their first steps, when they get straight As in school, when they graduate, and so on. We never grow out of wanting recognition, and survey after survey bears out that point.

For instance, a survey of 3,000 workers asked, "What do you really want from your job?" The top four answers were (in order of importance): 1. Career/learning/development opportunities, 2. Recognition, 3. Pay, and 4. Communication. In other words, these workers ranked recognition more important than money. Another study of 20,000 employees showed that companies with effective recognition efforts have a lower turnover rate, achieve better business results, and are strong in goal-setting, communication, trust, and accountability.

No doubt about it, recognition motivates people and feeds them on a deeper level. That's why it's important for business owners and leaders to understand and study team recognition. When you acknowledge team members—whether they're in sales, operations and even leadership—you show that you appreciate their efforts and value their contributions. Team members who are never recognized can become discouraged, unproductive and disgruntled. In the worst cases, they leave your company to find more rewarding employment elsewhere. Don't let your company be the type that allows its team to go unrecognized.

A Recognition Primer

All recognition is not the same and some types are better than others. In general, recognition is most effective when it comes from a company's highest level, but even mid- to lower-level leadership can have a huge impact on an organization simply by acknowledging the contributions of their team members. As long as your goal is to recognize people in a positive way for their achievements, you really can't go wrong. Here are some common types of recognition, with notes on when to use them.

On the spot. This type recognizes behavior, work ethic or leadership in a specific occurrence, either when it happens or a short time later. The value is enhanced when given in front of co-workers. At the same time, I'm a big fan of giving written notes someone can stash away and look at again and again. I have many and I send many.

Goal-related. This rewards an individual or team that reaches a measurable goal. To add a personal touch to the giving, learn what type of reward each individual would most appreciate. For instance, if a person is family oriented, reward them with something the entire family can enjoy.

Service/retirement. These awards recognize milestones in a life and/or career. Leadership could post the event in a prominent place—such as on a corporate bulletin board—and, ideally, present the award in an official manner. A meeting or luncheon, for example, is a great time to announce a service or retirement award. It is a very empty feeling to leave a company after many years of service without a shout out of some sort from leadership.

Personal. These recognitions acknowledge personal life events, such as birthdays. Again, post these prominently.

Companywide. Corporate events such as buying a department lunch, holiday parties or picnics are great ways to engage and acknowledge your team while having some fun in the process. Be creative and remember that you don't have to do the same thing every year.

Companies with a good human resource department might already have such programs in place. If your company doesn't, ask one of your administrative team members to manage at least the service award and birthday program—and don't forget to recognize that person if he or she does a good job. Make sure there is a committee who discusses and plans to create a memorable experience. If you don't know where to start, do a internet search on team recognition. There are pages of ideas with books and articles on the subject.

One of my close friends knows how to do the recognition thing right. One corridor in her company's facility has flags hanging from the ceiling representing every team member's country of origin to honor their heritage. Such touches explain why her team is genuinely happy to work there and why she has so many long-term employees. According to my friend, if new hires make it past 90 days in her company, they become "lifers." She isn't making that up: The president of her company was once a salesperson; the plant manager started in shipping and receiving. Her success is based on a strategic approach to running a business, but also the constant investment in—and recognition of—the teams personal and professional development.

Countering the anti-recognizers

In a Wichita State University (Wichita, Kansas) poll, only one in five workers recalled ever being recognized publicly at work, and fewer than half had received even one personal "thank you" from leadership. That raises the question: Why do companies consistently fail to recognize their teams? Given all the positive benefits of doing so, you'd think they would be falling over themselves to be appreciative of their people. To answer that question, I've discussed recognition with numerous levels of leadership, and I've heard all sorts of excuses for why they don't do it, including:

- "Why should they be recognized for what I'm paying them to do?"
- "I don't want to play favorites."
- "If I recognize them, they'll ask for more money."
- "If I recognize them too much, the recognition will lose its meaning."

Think they need some leadership training?

The way I see it, there's no legitimate reason not to recognize teams for their personal and professional accomplishments. Think about it: When you're at a sporting event or concert, you don't hold your praise and encouragement. When you see or hear something spectacular, you respond with cheers and applause throughout the event, recharging the athletes. In the same way, recognition engages, inspires and motivates your team; improves their morale; and helps retain the high performers, all while filling a basic human need.

Chapter Takeaway:

CHAPTER 30 | THE RIGHT CLOTHES TO CLOSE

Being known for what you know or what you wear

After a speaking engagement for the Chicago Chapter of the Association of Women in the Metal Industries in Oak Brook, Illinois, I stopped by the hotel bar for a beverage and feedback on my talk. The folks there—both female and male—gave my presentation a big thumbs-up. With the kudos flying, I decided to linger for a second drink. After a while, the group thinned out to five stragglers and the ladies present started reminiscing about the old days. We talked about the pioneering women in the metal industries, the challenges of working in a male-dominated industry, and the importance of how we represented ourselves and our companies—and of course what we wore. Most (though not all) of us wore business suits or slacks for our sales calls. We made sure to dress conservatively so as not to draw attention to our gender. No one wanted to be called a "skirt."

"It was easier for the guys," I told my new friends, who included two young salesmen. The male competitors in my Chicagoland market only had to throw on a suit or sport coat to make their calls. Aside from selecting complementary colors for their shirt, tie and coat, the men had few fashion decisions to worry about when meeting a customer or prospect. They simply put on their "man uniform" and went to work. Saleswomen, of course, had much more complicated fashion decisions and more pressure to dress "appropriately."

Over the years, I've watched—in horror, I might add—the changing fashions among salespeople. Today the industry's fashion theme seems to be, "It's all about me and my comfort—image be damned." Salespeople justify this approach by saying, "I dress like my customers so they feel more comfortable during my visit." Uh huh. My reply is: "Let them dress for their job; you dress for yours."

These days, it isn't unusual for salespeople to wear jeans on sales calls, and not your old-fashioned (so to speak) blue jeans, but $200 jeans that are faded, torn and worn to within an inch of their lives. The men's shirts typically look wrinkled, as if they came straight out of the hamper instead of the closet. (I have visions of a salesman smelling the armpits to decide if he can wear the shirt a second or third time.) The women wear 3- to 4-inch heels to visit their industrial customers and prospects. When they do wear a business suit, they use cleavage as an accessory. Yes, I'm generalizing, but the trend toward overstated casual is undeniable and it raises many questions about what salespeople wear on the job and how that affects their professionalism and customers' views of them and their company.

A Fashion Experiment

The evening was getting late, and only three of us remained from the original group—two young salesmen and I. We debated whether the casual state of today's business attire hurts or helps careers. My view, I said, is that it hurts you unless you own the company or don't need to produce because you have an "in" with one of the company's owners. Call me old-fashioned (that phrase again), but if I go to work wearing jeans and a T-shirt—the outfit I wear to clean my garage—I'm not dressed to represent my company, or myself, in a positive way. At a glance, the leadership can justifiably assume that I didn't have any sales calls that day. If anyone important visits the office, it is likely I wouldn't be introduced. Why? Because I don't look like a professional. If you care enough about the company to dress nicely for your initial job interview, why go slouchy after you get the job?

As a social experiment, I challenged the two young salesmen to report to work for the next month dressed in sharp, professional attire. Leave the comfy weekend clothes in the drawer; instead, dress each day like a professional going on a big sales call. My experiment, I hoped, would prove whether or not one's clothes make any difference. My chance, their challenge. After all, I've been wrong before.

The first week, they both dressed for success, but in the second week, one of the salesmen started wearing more casual attire. He was out. The other salesman was steadfast in his commitment, wearing a suit and tie every day. At first his more casually dressed colleagues harassed him. They asked relentlessly if he had a call—or a job interview. They began pressuring him to dress more like them. In turn, the leadership observed and made positive comments about his attire. After six months, I can report that the salesman enjoyed huge success. He had made more appointments and closed more business than ever before. His sales call-to-closing ratio increased substantially. His status moved to that of a professional. Dressing sharply, he told me, kept him focused on his job. He got it.

The lesson from my experiment? You don't dress professionally to impress others or fit into preconceived notions of what a professional is supposed to look like. You dress professionally because it affects how you feel about yourself and your job and because, in a work environment, it's the right thing to do. When you dress well, you present yourself, your job, and—most important—your company in the best possible light.

The "Comfortable Clothes" Syndrome

When training salespeople, I advise them to wear clothes in business that would be appropriate to wear to their grandmother's funeral. That usually eliminates the nose rings, jeans with holes in the knees, flashy high heels, and tube tops (though not always—some people just have no fashion sense, in the office or at the funeral home). If you'll be traipsing around industrial settings on a sales call, no, you don't have to wear your Armani suit or Manolo Blahnik shoes, but you still should look professional. And if your calls are to office settings, I still don't think I would "over-dress." Most prospects/customers don't choose to work with a salesperson because they wear expensive shoes or designer clothing. It's because they like and trust you. I tell young professionals, "You can be known for what you wear or what you know. Pick one."

In closing, a simple shout out to leadership: If your salespeople wear clothes that would be suitable for cleaning out the garage, you might want to check how many actual sales calls they've made in the past six months. I'd also look to see what business they've lost. It's my opinion that when they get too comfortable in their clothes, they also get too comfortable in their chairs.

Chapter Takeaway:

CHAPTER 31 | GIVING THANKS

Gratitude is good for the soul

When was the last time you gave a handwritten thank-you note to one of your colleagues? If you answer, "Just last week," then three cheers for you and you can skip this chapter. On the other hand, if you answered, "Never"—then read on to understand why such simple acknowledgements can make a huge difference in your success—and the success of your company.

Every Job Is Important

You can't overestimate how invested people get in their jobs and how important "attaboys" (and "attagirls") are to their overall job satisfaction and performance. According to Patrick Lencioni, author of *The Three Signs of a Miserable Job*, three factors that would make teams happier in their positions are

• Being known—in other words, acknowledgement from leadership and co-workers
• Relevance—getting confirmation that they make a difference
• Measurement—having a guideline on which to base their success

I saw a play that reinforced these points. The play, *Working,* is based on the 1974 Studs Turkel book *Working: People Talk About What They Do All Day and How They Feel About What They Do.* During the performance, characters describe their jobs, what their vocations mean to them, and how their work applies to the audience members' lives. After the play, I had a greater respect for each of the jobs as well as an understanding of their importance in the big picture. I understood better why every time an ironworker drives past a skyscraper on which he worked, he feels pride about his contributions to that structure. The same goes for the building's architect, plumber and window washer. The building is a physical reminder of their accomplishments, and they are proud of their parts in the ultimate success of that project.

In all industries, it's equally true that every job is important—from truck drivers to equipment operators, clerks to accounting departments, administrators to logistics, information systems to marketing, safety supervisors to salespeople, and many others. The fact is that each person needs the others to achieve success. All individuals and departments must work together to have any hope of achieving growth and success in the long run. It's a classic case of symbiotic relationships. Together we succeed; divided we fail.

This relationship dynamic is easy to see on the sales side. Salespeople are essential to a company's growth. Without sales, a company just exists—and maybe not for that long. A company can remain static and even survive the loss of an account or two, but any firm that wants to grow needs a strong sales professional or sales team retaining existing accounts and bringing in new business. Here's the rub, though: Without the support of the company's entire team, the salespeople would have nothing to sell.

Everything you market about your company—service, competitive pricing, technology, certifications, ingenuity and the like—is tied to your co-workers. Sure, you might secure a new customer on your own, but delivering what the customer expects is a team effort. From the person who answers the phone when your customer calls, to the person who manages the financial transactions, to those who support every aspect of the sale, it's their performance that will determine whether you keep the account. That's why it's so important to establish and maintain solid, supportive internal relationships with all of your colleagues.

Making Time For Thanks

What does all of this relationship talk have to do with handwritten thank-you notes? A lot, actually. A positive company culture encourages workers to have respect for and support their team members. A lot of it comes down to communication and thank-you notes are an extremely personal, supportive type of communication. Good communication keeps a company relating positively to each other and moving forward. Poor communication creates resentment and divisions between individuals and departments.

I've heard people describe a colleague as "just a laborer" and "a lazy salesperson." (At a recent conference, an officer of the company called his salespeople "stupid and lucky.") This type of disrespect is a clear sign the individual has no clue that his or her success—and the company's success—depends on that team member's contributions. That attitude flows through an organization like a virus. Once a company is infected, it takes great effort to treat and recover.

So I ask you this: What kind of co-worker are you? Do you...

• Respect all of your fellow workers?
• Make eye contact and say hello?
• Offer a cold drink to your colleagues who work outside on hot days?
• Bring lunch to co-workers who are working on a project that doesn't allow them to take a break?

- Take time to celebrate someone else's accomplishments instead of your own?
- Write thank-you notes to your colleagues, recognizing their contributions to your success?

"But there's too much to do, too many people to thank," you say. "Who has the time to do all that back-slapping? They're just doing their jobs, right?" Here's a heads-up: Smart salespeople make the time to thank the people who support them. Such efforts don't have to be expensive. A simple thank-you note, an email or an encouraging conversation is a positive (and inexpensive) way to recognize those who are the foundation of your success. I recently acknowledged an entire department merely by asking for their input on a new process. They gave me great ideas and I gave them methods for implementing the new procedures. My line of communication and relationship with this department is better than ever. So make a difference. Set a goal to write thank-you notes to five co-workers each month. I'm confident the practice will become a positive experience for your colleagues—and for you.

Chapter Takeaway:

CHAPTER 32 | LEADING FOR OTHERS' SUCCESS (OR, THANK YOU KENT)

Unleashing the potential in others

In August of 2011, I received the National Gold Award for regular contributed column from the American Society of Business Publication Editors (Wheaton, Illinois). That award was a career highlight for me, and a quite unexpected one. Winning an award for writing (or anything else) was never on my radar screen. Someone else—namely, the publisher and editor-in-chief of the magazine—placed it there. Totally unknown to me, he entered my *On Sales* column in the ASBPE article competition, and I somehow emerged the national winner. Go figure.

This heady incident got me thinking about leadership in general. It also made me reflect on varying leadership approaches, including my own, and how they can affect the career paths of those working with them.

Styles and Substance

I remember my first stab at sales in the scrap industry. I was a thirsty sponge with the desire to soak up as much knowledge in as little time as possible. I learned quickly and took to the recycling business like cream cheese to a bagel. I found the best way to navigate and communicate within the company and I strived to do my best. I wanted to be the No. 1 salesperson, not only at my company but in all of Chicago (my market at the time). Though I believe each of us has control over the level of success we achieve, I also believe that the right leadership, guidance and encouragement can contribute to that success. With good leadership, anything is possible—even something as unlikely as a sales professional winning a business writing award.

Throughout my career, I've heard salespeople describe leadership with every adjective in the book, including: fun, strict, inconsistent, nonexistent, helpful and some unprintable terms. Few, however, tell me stories about how anyone helped them reach unexpected heights of achievement and catapulted them to be champions in their industry. Great leadership creates top performers in their field. Regrettably, not all are endowed with the ability to selflessly move their team forward. In short, not everyone is cut out to be a great leader. There are as many leadership styles as there are leaders, but I've noticed a few broad categories in my career. The type of leader you get can mean the difference between excelling and languishing in the status quo.

Shoot-from-the-hip leadership. This type of leader tends to react to a situation quickly and with a lot of force, without thinking about the possible effects of his or her actions. Forget consistency—every day, week, month and year is different. People can't count on such leaders to provide much support because every day is a challenge for them. They're used to chaos and their teams get used to operating in that same state. This approach may be exciting due to its unpredictability, but it's terribly frustrating for those who want a steadier hand at the wheel.

Job-security leaders. My strategy in every job is to train my replacement. Doing so gives you the freedom to move into other roles in the company. I learned this at one of my high school jobs. I was passing out plastic numbers in a dressing room at a clothing store, and I aspired to be selling the clothes on the retail floor. I trained another employee to assume my dressing room position, allowing me to pursue sales. Leaders who are concerned about job security will never train their replacement. They also won't work to move you to the next level because they worry you'll leave them in the dust or worse, take their job. They provide the bare minimum in terms of knowledge so their teams are reliant on them. It's all about insecurity and control. These so-called leaders also find it difficult to ask for help, even if they're buried and they rarely give anyone credit for a job well done.

Roadblock leadership. This happens when a company moves people into a leadership role without training them how to be effective in that position. Instead, they have to learn as they go. The usual result? A person who doesn't function as a leader and stifles everyone working on their team. The company then has an immovable object in the corporate hierarchy. Can you imagine a doctor, lawyer or lion tamer learning as they go in their respective jobs? Of course not. So why do companies assume leaders can learn as they go? Sure, there are natural leaders, but even they know they can improve with training and they pursue it. It's baffling to me why we send unequipped people into the world of leadership when training is available and affordable. If you interview for a sales position, ask the interviewer what the company offers in terms of training for the leadership and sales team. No training means a stagnant workplace that will continue operating the way it always has.

Hitting the Trifecta

By now, you've deduced that finding a good leader isn't easy. That's why team members will sometimes follow a good leader when that person changes companies. When you find a leader who shares his or her knowledge, supports your success, and provides continuous training, you've hit the trifecta. There's no end to what you can learn or achieve. Such leaders have your back and empower you to make your own decisions. They provide opportunities for you to expand your own breadth of knowledge and encourage you to mentor others. When their team succeeds, they silently pat themselves on the back for choreographing yet another job well done.

I've been fortunate to work for great leaders throughout my career, people who have mentored and coached me to the next level. I've certainly tried to do that for others through my own leadership style and employee development seminars. Though I've stumbled through a few bad leadership moments, I learned what not to do from them and moved on. I won my writing award because my publisher submitted my columns for consideration. He believed I could accomplish something I'd never dreamed of and helped me reach a plane I didn't even know existed. With that type of leadership, anything is possible.

Chapter Takeaway:

_____

_____

_____

CHAPTER 33 | A RANT ON POOR WRITTEN COMMUNICATION

You were taught, you didn't listen

I admit I'm a stickler about written business communication. Without doubt, we all learned this in school, which is why it drives me crazy when I receive business letters that do not follow recognizable, acceptable formats. I see red when business correspondence is rife with typos and grammatical errors, and don't even get me started about way-too-casual business emails. "Ya" is not a professional answer to questions, and "Hey!" is no way to start business correspondence. When a young salesperson sent me an email that contained textspeak—abbreviations and acronyms instead of words—I headed straight to my computer to lay down some home truths about what's professional and, more important, what does not make me LOL (textspeak for "laugh out loud"). For months I thought it meant "lots of luck". Someone has to hold the line, after all.

The Right Format Matters

First, a little internal assessment might be in order. If you haven't done so, review your sales team's letters and proposals. You might be surprised by what you find and I can almost guarantee you'll be horrified if you peruse their emails. When I review letters and presentations in my sales consulting work, I leave few unchanged. Most of the time, such communications are written poorly and presented in unprofessional formats. I'm a huge proponent of using appropriate business letter writing styles. Most salespeople don't arrive at your company with letter writing expertise, which means their business communications usually don't follow standard formats. Instead, they write exactly as they speak or text. Further, most business correspondence goes out with mistakes because people rely on spell-check and don't proofread their work.

Fortunately, there are a couple of easy ways to address format deficiencies in business communications. First, your company could standardize its correspondence and keep a library of letters, proposals and presentations as a reference for salespeople to use when writing to their customers and prospects. I suggest spending a few dollars to hire a professional to write the documents, and then allow your salespeople to add their own verbiage to personalize them as desired. This approach gives your company some assurance that all written communications are consistent and professional.

Another option is to purchase a few books on business letters for your company library. Having three or four such books can help your sales team, administrative staff or anyone else needing a reference for letter writing purposes. The book I have in my office has samples of more than 1,000 letter styles. And needless to say, you can find almost anything online.

The Trouble With Textspeak

My biggest complaint about today's business communications is the use of textspeak in emails and even printed letters. Now, don't get me wrong. I'm not a Luddite who wants to ban texting from the face of the earth. I'm a fan of texting, in fact. I find it's a wonderful way to communicate with teenagers because it's short and sweet, and it eliminates their whining and eye-rolling. There's no denying that texting has made electronic written communications shorter, which isn't bad in itself. Who doesn't appreciate brevity? The downside is when textspeak reduces the written word to abbreviations that resemble a foreign language, or code from an alien race. When receiving an email from a young salesperson—the entire text of which was "ompl," followed by a smiley face—I had to enlist the assistance of a thirtysomething translator to decipher the code. That abbreviation, I learned, means "one moment, please." As for the smiley face, I can only assume it meant she was tickled by the thought of our pending email communication. (If you don't have a thirtysomething translator handy, fear not; you can consult www.urbandictionary.com to answer your electronic communication question or just Google any abbreviation.)

In my view, textspeak has no place in communications with customers and prospects. It's especially important to communicate that message to the multi-texters—those who engage in two or three text conversations while sitting in meetings. I've also noticed, with chagrin, that textspeak is crossing over into other communications, especially email. When using a smartphone, it's easy to switch from texting to emailing, and—intentionally or not—we can too easily start using textspeak in the reply. When the recipient views the email on a computer, the textspeak-filled email will stand out from other messages, and not in a good way. Such abbreviated language challenges the reader, who can misinterpret your point, assume you're illiterate or has indication that you don't know Text from Email on your smart phone. No joke, I have seen "u" instead of "you" in a written thank you note if that tells you where we are heading. Tell your team to save the textspeak for personal communications and refrain from using it with customers and prospects. I was recently asked by my son in college not to use "thot" as an abbreviation for "thought" in a text. I asked why and he told me in his world it meant "that whore over there." My response was "omg."

Nix the Emoticons Already

While I'm on my rant, I'm also not crazy about the combinations of symbols, numbers and letters that create pictures or emoticons. I have received those doo-dahs in scores of business-related correspondence. I didn't like the smiley face in the 1970s and I especially don't like it now in professional emails or texts. Yes, the graphics are ingenious, cute, and playful, but they have no place in business communication. Save them for your friends who weren't around in the 1970s.

As technology progresses, I'll continue to take advantage of any new efficiencies it offers. At the same time, I'll always believe in the power and importance of a formal business document. Taking the time to create a business letter, proposal or written thank-you note tells your customers or prospects they're worthy of your time and energy. Beginning that correspondence with the "Dear … " salutation rather than "Hey" is icing on the cake.

And when closing an email or in written correspondence, I would veer towards not abbreviating and keeping it as professional as possible. I read an article called *57 Ways to Sign Off on an Email* (www.forbes.com/sites/susanadams/2013/09/27/ 57-ways-to-sign-off-on-an-email) that I find to be helpful in training situations.

Serious business correspondence need words with professionalism and content. What if our national leaders had been just as casual about their communications over the years? They might have come up with the following, which I found while conducting a Google search about texting:

"i plj alejns 2 th flg, of th untd sts of amrca. n 2 th rpblc 4 whch it stnds; 1 ntn, ndr gd, ndvsbl, wth lbrty n jstc 4 all!"

That puts it all into perspective, doesn't it? If this doesn't make you want to review your sales team's written communications, I don't know what will.

Chapter Takeaway:

CHAPTER 34 | MEETINGS MAKE THE DIFFERENCE

Gathering teams to communicate effectively

I've attended the opening day game of the Chicago White Sox for more than three decades. Opening Day is like a holiday for me—my favorite holiday in fact (sorry, Santa). One year while I was at the game, I called the office to check in with my team. The phone rang and rang, but no one answered. When I finally reached someone on her cell phone, I learned that no one answered because no one was there. It seems the company closed early to enjoy my Sox Opener holiday too. I learned a couple of lessons that day: 1. be specific in communicating the expected protocol while I'm away from the office, and 2. team members follow the leader. Opportunity knocked and my team answered the door.

Such instances usually boil down to a failure to communicate. When there's a lack of communication in the workplace, there eventually follows a lack of understanding that inhibits growth, continuity, and success. There are many ways to communicate, but I believe meetings can be an extraordinary method for connecting the dots. Those of you who don't like meetings need to get over it, just as you got over your distaste for homework or Brussels sprouts. Without meetings, people are left to do what they think they should be doing—or what they want to do (as my team did)—rather than what you are expecting them to do.

Salespeople need leadership to thrive and survive and meetings are an excellent way for the sales leader to communicate with the team. Meetings are where you set goals, inform them of company accomplishments, share industry knowledge, and develop sales strategies. Without meetings your sales team will flail about and team members can become needy, uninformed, unprepared and disconnected. What follows are suggestions to improve your meeting mojo:

Start with a plan. An agenda is essential for a successful meeting. It's your road map, charting the path that keeps you on course and prevents you from facilitating the "way too long meeting from hell". I keep a running list of agenda items in a folder on my computer, but a manila folder works, too— whichever approach helps you focus on specifics. To create the agenda, I simply prioritize the items on my list and insert them into one of the meeting agenda templates I find on the internet. It's important to create a timeline for your meeting that defines a specific block of time for each agenda item. Making the items time-bound prevents one item from consuming too much of the meeting. After drafting the agenda, forward it to your team members so they can be prepared with any necessary materials and ideas. Reviewing the timeline makes it clear that specific topics are only open for discussion for specific time slots.

Stay on topic. A common complaint about meetings is they often swerve off topic, a phenomenon that makes most everyone frantic with frustration. Remember, attending a meeting is only one item on everyone's to-do list that day, so it's respectful to stay on task. A good meeting leader will keep the meeting focused by using phrases like: "That's a good point, but let's discuss it after the meeting," or "I appreciate your concern; we can talk about that later, one on one." Whatever words you choose, the goal is to bring the attendees back to the agenda and stop them from wasting time.

Minimize distractions. Strive to eliminate distractions and disruptions from your meetings. It's difficult for anyone to stay focused if people are wandering in and out, or if individuals are taking phone calls or reading emails in the middle of the gathering. You're running a professional meeting, not a Montessori school, so everyone in the room needs to focus on the subject at hand. Do all you can to avoid the Sister Mary Elephant situation in a meeting. (Google it, it's funny)

Focus on work, not personal attacks. Some salespeople dislike meetings because the gatherings become attacks on their team performance or individual team members. Such meetings are demeaning, debilitating, and counterproductive. Afterward, the salespeople scrape what's left of their self-esteem off the floor and mope back to their desks to spend time griping or surfing the web for a new position. Meetings are tools to achieve better and more professional performance, not forums to turn your salespeople into disgruntled, unproductive teams.

Avoid "whatchagot" meetings. A "whatchagot" meeting is one where leadership expects the sales team to come with morsels of information to share. Familiar topics often include gossip about the competition or complaints about another department. The lazy leader likes these meetings because they require no preparation or leadership on their part. They wait to hear what the salespeople say and then improvise a response. This type of meeting is unproductive and often negative. There's nothing like a room full of negative comments to fire up your crew. The alternative is to start planning your meetings (see "Start with a plan," above) and show your team "whatchugot," which shows you care enough to share your own information and don't expect them to do all the heavy lifting.

The Case for Meetings

If you're the anti-meeter—one who absolutely, positively detests group meetings—the only alternative is to meet individually with each salesperson. While there is definitely a place for one-on-one communication, it should not be your principal method. Such an approach is exclusive rather than inclusive and wastes valuable time and energy. Some team members might see you spending more time with one or more of their peers and feel left out. It's also easy to give inconsistent information from one person to the next because it's difficult to remember what was said to whom. It's like taking everyone in your family on the same vacation individually—it's highly inefficient and fraught with potential problems.

Instead, I encourage everyone—especially the anti-meeters—to begin every year with a meeting. Recap last year's sales activity and review the company's expectations for the year ahead. Enlist the team's help in setting the company's sales goals. Ask your team to set his or her personal goals. Goals are important. Without them, people have no target. It's like playing basketball without the basket. Share market information, industry articles, company accomplishments, and initiatives that will affect the team's success. Most of the sales team will feel more connected and motivated after a sales meeting. What then? Pick a date to meet again, at least once a month. Over time, meetings can make the difference between a knowledgeable, cohesive sales team and an uninformed, divisive group. Which would you rather have?

Chapter Takeaway:

CHAPTER 35 | THE REWARDS OF PAYING IT FORWARD

Sharing your expertise with others...just because

I well remember the year my husband and I visited universities with our son. At one school in Illinois, a sophomore marketing major named Elizabeth led the campus tour. In addition to being enthusiastic, she was informed and familiar with every part of the campus. During the tour, I pulled her aside and asked in a hushed tone: "Is there a lot of partying here on the weekends?" I wanted to know because my son didn't receive my "party gene." He preferred a quieter, less chaotic environment. "Well," she replied, "I'm not going to say no. If you're looking for a party, you can find one, but there are plenty of students who aren't like that." I immediately thought this young woman would be great in a sales position. She was knowledgeable, honest and tactful.

During the tour, I shared with her that I work in sales and marketing. Her eyes lit up and she later asked if she could contact me. I gave her my business card, fully expecting her to use it to wrap old gum and file it in the trashcan. But a couple of days later, she sent me an email and followed up with a phone call asking if we could meet on campus so she could "pick my brain." Due to my travel demands and general work overload, I had no available time to meet her during the next few weeks. After a month passed, she sent me another email and again followed up with a call. I was still too busy to see her.

Soon thereafter, my son decided to visit Elizabeth's school for a second time, so I resolved to give her a call and find the time to meet with her. Despite my best intentions, I again became distracted with work. On the day of our second visit, a politely determined Elizabeth sent me an email and called to see when I'd be available, so I immediately scheduled a meeting with her at the campus coffee shop. I was impressed by her ability to be persistent without being a nudge and her impeccable timing—two more successful sales characteristics.

I found Elizabeth waiting for me at a table in the coffee shop. She had a notebook of information she'd extracted from my website and a list of open-ended questions about my career in sales and marketing. She was very punctual, informed and prepared.

Our meeting lasted more than an hour. It was an important hour of my life for several reasons. First, I was enthused to think that this college, where my husband and I would spend a good portion of our life savings, played at least some part in teaching Elizabeth the skills of a business professional by her sophomore year. Our hard-earned money would be well spent there. Second, her questions reminded me of my sales journey that led to the accomplishments I now take for granted. Most important, our meeting reminded me to get back to one of my career goals—devoting time to career guidance programs and mentoring students in their chosen fields.

Walking the Mentoring Path

In a previous chapter I discussed volunteering for a mentoring program several years ago where I was paired with a high school junior named Katie. We still keep in touch. She landed a marketing job at a large not-for-profit organization, which allows me to tap into her knowledge of social media and digital marketing. Despite my great mentoring experience with Katie, I didn't think to find another protégé after her. I became wrapped up in my training and consulting career. Though my day-to-day work offered some mentoring opportunities, it wasn't as gratifying as personally guiding a student who is exploring new possibilities and career choices.

Most professionals are in the same boat, I know—too busy with their daily duties to spend time mentoring. That's a huge loss, not only for students or young professionals seeking career guidance but also for we business professionals who have so much to offer. After all, the best way to learn is by teaching. I know many business professionals who have much to offer from a variety of disciplines including: sales, marketing, operations, finance, human resources, technology and entrepreneurship. Everyone has stories to tell and knowledge to share.

I also know from personal experience that most people are incredibly generous and I hope this chapter prompts at least some of you to ask, "How can I get involved?" A good start is identifying your professional knowledge areas and then creating a summary document or presentation. Next, call a local high school or college and ask whether they have any classes or student groups that could benefit from your knowledge. If you're a sales and marketing professional, you could share your experience and perspective with students in a marketing or business class. It's invaluable for students to understand that what they're learning in the classroom really applies to the workplace. Many schools would welcome your offer and connect you with an instructor in the appropriate field.

After my meeting with Elizabeth, I connected her to experts in the sports marketing and advertising agency sectors. She invited some of these professionals to participate in a series of panel discussions organized through the college's sales and marketing organization. I also connected Elizabeth to Katie through social media. I'm sure Katie will give her valuable guidance as well. Elizabeth and I also spent time reviewing her professional strengths, which I think helped her realize the many opportunities available.

No doubt many of you have your own mentoring stories, so I don't have to sell you on the rewards. But for those of you who haven't yet shared your time and knowledge in this way, I encourage you to "pay it forward." I guarantee you won't regret it.

Chapter Takeaway:

_____

_____

_____

CHAPTER 36 | LEARNING FROM YOUR OWN MISTAKES

Admitting and sharing to protect the innocent

I'll never forget my most awkward moment in sales. I was visiting an manufacturing plant in Wisconsin on a frigid December morning. The receptionist escorted me to the office of my contact who happened to be a man in a wheelchair. I had only spoken with him by phone, so this discovery threw me, but I gamely stuck out my hand in greeting. He ignored it. I offered my hand a second time. He ignored it again. Puzzled but not deterred, I tried once more, and he relented. He lifted his arm and held out a prosthetic hand fixed with stainless steel hook. I shook it—what else could I do? But I've never completely forgiven myself for that dreadful moment. Lesson learned: If someone doesn't shake your hand immediately, he or she probably has a good reason.

In another embarrassing incident, I was in a prospect's office and noticed a photo of a young woman. "Your daughter is beautiful," I said. "That's my girlfriend," he replied. Note to self: Commenting on personal photos is dangerous territory.

All salespeople commit *faux pas* at some time in their career. My sales cronies and I regale each other with our past blunders including: bringing glazed donuts to a diabetic customer, burping not once, but twice, during a presentation, and the favorite: leaving a wallet at home and having to ask a prospect for toll money. All of these gaffes are forgivable, even endearing, but any sane salesperson would prefer not to make them. We can learn from our own and others' mistakes and minimize the chances of future embarrassment by remembering some sales call basics:

Be prepared. The Girl/Boy Scout motto is just as relevant in sales situations. Though I've been trained in improvisation, I know the risks of winging it on sales calls and I don't do it. Instead, I always carry a list of "small talk" questions, usually based on research I've done on the company and/or contact. While you can always look for conversational cues in a prospect's office or facility for starters, I recommend doing your homework in advance. Corporate websites and social media offer an abundance of intelligence on prospective customers. Virtually every company's website has an "About Us" section. Internet and social media searches can provide information on a company and its teams. In short, the internet makes it easy to prep for a sales call and be "in the know" long before you pull into the visitor parking space. If you're a sales dinosaur still clinging to your fax machine instead of taking advantage of these resources, jump aboard my friend, or risk going the way of the T. Rex.

Keep it professional. When I make a sales call, I do my best to assess the prospect's personality type and avoid conversations that could lead to uncomfortable exchanges. In my view, there's no place for politics, religion, or flirting in business conversations. Behaving professionally is essential. I've been on sales calls where prospects and/or salespeople have lost their cool and become antagonistic. Give and take is good; sparring is bad; flirting is really bad. I tell the story of a young salesman who told me about his flirtatious phone calls with a female customer. This was before social media took over. When the two finally met face to face, she did not live up to his expectations in the looks department. He lost the account—and entered himself in the running for the World's Most Shallow Person Award. His example is a good reminder why it's essential to be professional.

Always follow up. In my book, poor follow-up is the worst professional blunder a salesperson can make. It's the fastest way to turn a good sales call into a bad relationship. If you promise to send additional information or a proposal, do it immediately. The prospect will view your prompt follow-up as an indication of your future responsiveness. If you follow up after an appointment without scheduling another meeting or conversation, don't be surprised when you don't get a response. Ask prospects about their preferred form of communication and how frequently to contact them in the future. That's more productive than spamming them with phone calls and emails, which can be good way to alienate anyone.

After you close a sale, find out exactly what your customers expect going forward. Do they want to see you weekly, monthly, quarterly or never? Do they want you to send them business articles and publications? Are they interested in lunch, golf or a baseball game? Don't get complacent after signing a contract. Capturing an account and forgetting about it leads to lost accounts. The old saying "out of sight, out of mind" rings true as you'll quickly learn when you answer the call to cancel your service.

Don't burn bridges. All sales professionals lose accounts during their careers. No one likes it but it happens for legitimate reasons including competitor pressure and changing business conditions. Many companies bend over backward to retain accounts, sometimes by charging less or succumbing to absurd requests for added services like paying the customer's refuse bill or donating bicycles to picnics of multimillion-dollar corporations. One customer asked me to give him a theater subscription in order to keep his company's account (I did not oblige.) When business relationships end, it's important to end them on a positive note. After all, you never know when you'll run into old customers at a new company and you might get an opportunity to win back their business in the future.

Even after 30 years in sales, I still have (occasional) embarrassing moments when I could have used better words, responded in a better way, prepared more, improved my follow up and occasionally lost a deal. We're all busy people and none of us is perfect. As long as you learn from your mistakes and stay current with new technology, you can reach your sales goals and avoid future *faux pas.*

Chapter Takeaway:

CHAPTER 37 | A TIMELINE FOR CAREER SUCCESS

Mapping out your career decade by decade

I once read an article in *Money* magazine titled *Make Your Money Last and Last* offered a timeline of financial guidance and goals for individuals based on ages ranging from 20 to 70. According to the article, your early 40s are the optimal time to gear up your career. I agree with the whole career-planning and milestone-setting process, but I maintain that aspiring sales professionals need to work ahead of the curve outlined in the article. Here's my stab at a decade-by-decade timeline for those interested in succeeding in a sales career.

If You're in Your 20s

Your 20s can be the perfect time to embark on a sales career—if you're organized, focused, motivated and polished. People in their 20s often lack professional experience that prevents them from excelling in sales. Case in point: One salesman in his late 20s opted out of one of my sales training workshops because he had received some training at his previous job (he now denies that). It is my opinion that people who choose not to refresh or expand their professional knowledge are headed for one place—mediocrity. These people might have had a few good years in sales, but continuing education is essential to reach the next level. Your 20s are the perfect time to be a sponge for any type of learning. And with all the formats available, there is simply no reason to ignore or delay. Classroom education, on-the-job training, working with a mentor, independent reading, web-based training, newsletters, case studies and much more. The education you gain in your 20s is foundational as you enter your 30s and prepares you for future success in sales.

If You're in Your 30s

You're now well-versed in the sales process having solid experience in gathering and applying critical sales information in your daily routine. You also know what is necessary to succeed in your company. At this stage, you need to ask yourself several questions: Are you committed to your career in sales? Do you want to be the best in your sales niche? Is this the best industry for your talents? Are you passionate about what you sell? Do you need or want additional training or can you better apply education you've already received? Does your company offer opportunities for career growth? Is anyone in your company or industry helping you reach the next step? Have you begun attending industry functions and become active in social media to grow your network, raise your visibility, and acquire knowledge useful to your career?

Becoming the best in sales is extremely rewarding, but it takes work. Your 30s are a good decade to invest the necessary time and effort. One of my professional goals was to become so good in sales that companies in my industry would hire me without even needing to see my résumé. I achieved that goal in four years. I was on the fast track, but it took a lot of personal commitment and sacrifices. My friends were growing their children while I was growing my customer base.

When considering opportunities for career growth, entering leadership is one option, but remember it isn't for everyone. If you think you're interested in becoming a sales executive, ask whether you can shadow someone in leadership at your company to make sure the position is a good fit for you. That could save you a lot of heartache, frustration and career backpedaling later. And most of the time you can make more dollars and have fewer headaches in a straight sales role.

If You're in Your 40s

You now have deep knowledge of your industry, lots of contacts, and an excellent reputation in your market and related industries. If your current employer doesn't offer the growth opportunities you seek, don't waste time. Start interviewing— not only with companies in your industry but also with those in associated fields. A good friend of mine in her early 40s went from working for a scrap company to joining a consulting firm. She couldn't be happier. She earned her MBA in her 30s and is thrilled about the prospect of taking her industry knowledge to a new level. If you resist expanding your professional knowledge through additional training or education take note: people like my friend will eat your lunch in the future.

If You're in Your 50s and Early 60s

You're a pro by now, a true sales veteran who has seen and experienced it all. Your experience is your power. If you have managed to stay in the same industry, it's now time to start giving back through mentoring, involvement in industry trade associations, and helping your company plan its future. These activities are keys to your continued growth, both personally and professionally. I am in this age category and I enjoy working closely with young salespeople who never fail to teach me something new every day. Your industry associations have much to gain from your experience and perspective—so serve on a committee or research group at the local, national, or international level. You can save the younger leaders from having to reinvent the wheel by sharing your wisdom. Believe me, the younger generation will appreciate your contributions as long as you embrace their love for technology and don't bore them with stories about how things were before the emergence of the fax machine.

If You Have Changed Gears Somewhere Along the Way

Maybe you have gone from one type of sales to another or entered the sales field later in your career. All of the above are essential. Training in any way, shape or form is necessary to succeed. Just because you have reached success in one field doesn't set you up for an instant replay. I have another friend who spent the first part of his career in IT management selling hardware/software solutions and found the career transition to sales was not easy. Since he'd spent most of his career on the other side of the desk making purchasing decisions he suddenly found it difficult to ask for the sale as he feared being pushy or "salesy" as he called it. His previous position in no way prepared him for the repeated rejection of a sales career. But to a seasoned sales professional, rejection rolls off like water off a duck's back. No big deal. Move on. Cha, cha, cha.

If You're in Your Mid-60s and 70s

If you are fortunate enough to still be working in sales, you've earned the right to coast a bit now, maintaining and enjoying the customer base you worked so hard to create. If you're still bringing in new business, kudos to you! That's clear proof you are as passionate about your sales career today as ever before. I once asked a man in his 70s why he continued to report to work every day. His response: "If you knew my wife, you'd know why." That man worked until the day he died. I suspect his real reason for working so long was that he simply loved his job. Loving your job—the key to a timeless career in any field.

Chapter Takeaway:

CHAPTER 38 | IT'S ALL ABOUT THE FOLLOW-UP

Being organized in your approach

When you attend an event to establish new contacts, turning those contacts into prospects requires follow up. Yet, according to *Sales & Marketing Management* magazine, 80 percent of trade-show leads aren't turned into new business due to—what else? Poor follow up. As a sales professional, I find that unforgivable. There's nothing worse than having an interesting discussion with people at an event, telling them you'll call, and then failing to follow up. Anyone can gather business cards, but success depends on what you do with them afterward.

After attending an event, I strategize about how best to follow up with the people I met. My goal is to avoid having a pile of business cards gathering dust on my desk. You know the pile: some of the business cards are plain, without notes, and you can't remember why you even have them. Others have notes on them, but you can't remember what the scribble means because you didn't follow up right away or you wrote the notes after a couple of cocktails. After a month or two passes, you feel it's too late to call the prospect. But don't forget—each card represents a potential customer, so each one you don't pursue is a missed opportunity. You can capitalize on those opportunities by heeding a few follow-up steps.

Transforming Contacts Into Customers

For starters, I recommend observing some polite follow-up protocol. It's OK to ask prospects in person when to follow up, but if you don't do that, it is a good practice to give folks a week after a conference or tradeshow before calling. They usually need some time to catch up at the office. If you met at a networking event, you can follow up immediately. And obviously if you have a hot lead, make the call now—do not pass GO, do not collect two hundred dollars.

In the week after the event, while your prospects catch up at work, send written thank-you notes to any contacts who treated you to a nice meal or entertainment. Just like responding to an RSVP, it's the right thing to do and your contacts will remember your thoughtfulness and professionalism. Plus, when you follow up with them, they might be more receptive to your call as they glance at your handwritten note lying open on their desk.

After writing those notes, organize your business cards using whatever technology works for you. I use Contacts in Microsoft Outlook, organizing them into categories and then I flag the contact for follow up. The Flag is my friend. There are higher-tech approaches as well. I met someone at a convention who took a photo of my business card with his smartphone and digitized the information to his Contacts. It was slick. I took his lead and never looked back. I now use an app to capture business card information and eliminate cards from piling up on my desk. While I doubt printed business cards will become extinct, new timesaving devices and apps are available to record the information into your smart phone or computer and streamline the contact-management process. Literally, there is no excuse for poor follow up.

After a week has passed, it's time to contact your prospects. First, it's a nice touch to send each person an email indicating you plan to call soon. When you call, refer to your original conversation to jog the person's memory and re-establish your initial connection. It's easier to do this when you take some notes after your initial meeting. The goal is to create a solid, comfortable foundation for the next stage of your sales relationship.

The process is slightly different for companies that gather scores of business cards as exhibitors at trade shows. My best advice is to have one person contact all the prospects, then pass each lead to the appropriate sales rep. The call would go something like this: "Hi, my name is Judy from ABC Company. Thank you for stopping by our booth at the convention. Joe Rainmaker, one of our regional sales professionals spoke with you, and I'm calling to schedule a follow-up appointment. What date and time would work for you?" After making each appointment, the caller sends the information as a qualified lead to the appropriate salesperson who should follow up promptly to maintain the sales momentum.

Once the prospect is downloaded into your Contacts, you can flag that record for follow up on a certain day and time. When setting a reminder correctly, your device will notify you when to follow up. It is a beautiful thing. Anyone not using the many timesaving features in Outlook needs to know that communicating through email does not make you computer savvy, it just makes you normal.

And finally, don't underestimate the power of social media. Each contact made at any event should be fodder for LinkedIn. It will connect you immediately and alert your new connection when you post information, update your profile, or have a business anniversary. Social media is powerful and helpful so don't neglect using its full capacity.

The above suggestions aren't the only ways to follow up on sales leads. But be sure you follow up one way or another.

Chapter Takeaway:

_____

_____

_____

CHAPTER 39 | THE TWO SIDES OF ACCESSIBILITY

Being an available and reliable leader

Is leadership at your company accessible? I ask because I've noticed a disturbing trend lately—the growing inaccessibility of higher-level leadership. In conversations with numerous people, I've heard plenty of complaints about not having enough face time with leadership. They say department heads seem aloof, distant and detached from their teams. This makes individuals and teams feel "abandoned" and "unimportant." Those professionals aren't high-maintenance, unreasonable people—but strong, independent producers who claim they aren't getting guidance when needed. Such talk is a warning flag for any organization because it's a sign of a discontent culture. It's a problem when an organization has a handful of rainmakers complaining about a disconnect with leadership rather than producing. When one is disappointed in a relation-ship, there's a consequence. In this case, hours of productivity are wasted and valuable team members may consider leaving the company.

There are two sides to every issue. In defense of busy leaders, being too accessible has its drawbacks. It becomes difficult to talk with everyone and still get one's own work done. Fortunately, offering face time doesn't have to mean a long conversation. Leaders can learn to have a balance. One sales manager implemented a simple policy—door's open, come in. Door's closed, send an email or IM to talk later. There's a happy medium between being too accessible and nearly unavailable.

Out With The Bad

If you're a leader, you can improve your accessibility quotient by replacing certain bad work habits with good ones. Here are a few don'ts: Do not ignore emails, phone calls or requests for meetings from your team. Do not give time to some but not others. Do not accept invitations to meetings and then fail to show. When you accept meeting invitations, the team is looking forward to the meeting and your attendance. You need to be there! When you're a no-show you are clearly saying: I don't care.

On the flip side, I don't endorse a completely open-door policy because it isn't a feasible reality for busy leaders. That approach makes it difficult to achieve your own work objectives each day. When your door is always open only a small percentage of people take advantage of that privilege. You'll find yourself spending 80 percent of face time with only 20 percent of your team. The squeaky wheel gets the oil while the others rust.

In With The Good

To address any existing open-door problems, start tracking the time you spend with each person on your team. This helps you identify the high-maintenance time suckers and stalkers who hang around your office door. To better plan and manage your time, require everyone to make an appointment and bring an agenda for the meeting. You can change their behavior by changing yours.

On a less formal level, you can achieve a good accessibility balance by giving your team face time at a weekly or monthly team meeting or having an off-site breakfast or lunch where people can speak with you in a relaxed environment. Just make sure you have an agenda and strictly limit the meeting to one hour. In addition to keeping everyone informed, connected and moving in the same direction—regular team meetings reduce the need for one-on-one communication.

Lastly, don't neglect to respond to all correspondence from your team. It only takes a moment to respond, and every response is an affirmation that you care. Remember, avoidance is not a trait of a leader.

Striking the right accessibility balance is a challenge every leader must resolve based on the particular demands of the job. The challenges are significant; having potentially frustrated people on one side and overworked leaders on the other. Fortunately, it's possible to find the happy path with a little focus and concerted effort.

Chapter Takeaway:

CHAPTER 40 | THE ARGUMENT AGAINST SALES ON THE CHEAP

You get what you pay for

I've learned there are two types of companies when it comes to sales: those making an effort to support and invest in their sales teams and those trying to get a bargain by combining operational and sales responsibilities which forces their team to multitask.

I first saw this dichotomy while attending a peer group meeting nearly 20 years ago. A member of the group expressed interest in hiring a person for sales and marketing. He asked for my opinion, so I requested the position's job description. The new person, he said, would have to maintain current customers, increase sales, network in the industry, create and manage the company's website, develop marketing collateral, and a host of other tasks. "That's a job for three people," I said. My recommendation was to outsource the marketing work, hire someone for inside sales to manage and maintain his current customer base, and hire the sales professional to concentrate on growing the business. In the end, he didn't take my advice because he thought my approach would be more expensive. Instead, he spent more money hiring one person after another, none of whom could meet his unrealistic standards. High employee turnover is very expensive. You do the math.

That was not an isolated incident. Shortly thereafter, I spoke with two individuals who work for a large company. In addition to running different operational aspects of the business, they're expected to maintain the company's more than 500 accounts and bring in new business. I'll bet they spend 85 percent of their time on operational matters, 5 percent on maintaining accounts, 5 percent on developing new business, and 5 percent complaining how much they're overworked. Many companies cling to this outdated, pile-on approach to sales (and other positions) because they believe the status quo is fine. They think what worked in the past will continue to work in the future, but nothing is further from the truth. Today, the status quo approach is a surefire way to make your company less competitive and limit its potential growth—perhaps even send it on the road to extinction. If you need any motivation to change, imagine these scenarios:

1. A strong competitor decides to expand into your territory. Its salespeople begin calling on your accounts—you know, the ones your sales reps don't see very often because they're too busy juggling five other tasks. Those frustrated customers complain to competitor about your lack of attention and like any effective predator, they swallow the opportunity. The next thing you know, your customers are their customers.

2. Let's say that a new, young and hungry company enters your market, one that knows how to leverage today's technology. Its use of Google, Facebook, Twitter, LinkedIn, Instagram, SEO/SEM technologies and other media allows its salespeople to find and connect with your customers in ways you never imagined. They also know how to develop and implement an innovative, effective marketing plan to attract customers. You get involved much too late and find your customers have been successfully stalked and captured.

These scenarios have the following in common: they invest in directly developing their sales and marketing professionals. They don't expect their salespeople to spend time in operations, marketing, and wherever else you plug them. If you haven't modernized your approach, you'd better start looking over your shoulder because smarter, faster companies who love the word "outsource" are creeping up on you.

I'm very familiar with such scenarios. I've received more than one frantic call from small business owners asking what they should do when the "big guys" invade their turf. My first question is, "How many salespeople do you have?" More often than not, the owner is the only salesperson. I advise to focus immediately on protecting your company's current business, and hire a professional salesperson dedicated to building new business. The owner's next question is usually, "How would I manage a salesperson?"—which really means, "How would I micromanage a salesperson?" After I give them a crash course on how not to micromanage, and discuss what they can expect to pay for good talent, their knee-jerk reaction is to hire someone they already know. While that approach may work occasionally, it more often wastes time and creates dissention. Set ego and nepotism aside when hiring salespeople and focus instead on hiring the most capable individuals you can find.

Some companies like to hire from within which is short for "we can use this person to do sales and their old job." Doesn't work. Nothing worse for a company than to have a salesperson who is distracted by what is more comfortable for them, their old job.

Another common approach—one that makes me cringe—is hiring salespeople on commission only. That might represent the smallest risk for the company, but it's the least appealing approach for the salesperson. This is a short-term model that rarely works. I am in favor of a base salary for salespeople, you know, so they can live and buy milk and bread.

Making The Investment

When it comes to sales, my adage is "you get what you pay for". Companies who hire salespeople on the cheap can't realistically expect them to work above and beyond the call of duty by sacrificing their evenings to networking or entertaining clients. You simply won't get that commitment. Companies expecting fabulous results from salespeople without providing proper training are deluding themselves. Inexperienced salespeople take time to mature and build momentum; your company can help by hiring a trainer or consultant to give them the skills and leadership they need.

So, what can you, and should you, expect from your sales team? Here are a few pointers collected from my years in sales.

1. A competent salesperson can effectively manage 100 accounts based on the 80/20 rule, meaning 80 percent of the accounts should require minimal maintenance so the more demanding 20 percent get the attention they need.
2. If the salesperson is managing 100 or more accounts, the best way to keep him or her focused on adding new business is by offering incentives and/or bonuses.
3. Salespeople take better care of accounts they land themselves. If they must manage existing/house accounts, a retention bonus or bonus based on profitability of their entire account list can prompt them to care for those customers as their own.
4. By developing a compensation plan, your sales team will have a clear understanding of the process and spend less time trying to figure it out.
   • If your company has a sales team focused on new business and account maintenance, I recommend having someone in a dedicated sales support role. This provides customers with another contact in your organization and saves your salespeople from spending valuable time chasing paperwork, ordering promotional items, and generating reports for their customers.
   • If the salesperson is being hired to primarily maintain existing customers, the hiring process and qualifications will vary with the salary.

5. Great salespeople don't necessarily need to be promoted as much as they need to be praised and rewarded for their hard work.

Resist the temptation to manage your corporate sales on the cheap. Instead, consider sales a necessary and worthwhile investment in your company's future success. Rather than worrying about your sales efforts and constantly looking over your shoulder, you can have a sales program that keeps you well ahead of the competition.

Chapter Takeaway:

_____

_____

_____

CHAPTER 41 | ARE DIFFICULT TEAMS JUST POORLY LEAD?

Understanding the importance of communication styles, yours and theirs

When I was asked to speak at a conference, the association gave me a challenging assignment: Talk about dealing with difficult teams from the perspective that perhaps the team isn't necessarily at fault; maybe they just need better leadership. Always up for a challenge, I accepted the invitation and immediately enlisted an associate who had conducted numerous leadership seminars to help me develop the workshop. Our starting point was the advice of author Jim Collins.

> **Collins:** To operate effectively, we need "the right person, in the right seat, on the right bus, going in the right direction." Thus, our plan was to teach attendees how to hire the best team members—or get the right people on the right bus—and then facilitate exercises to help them effectively engage with their team members.

We started the workshop by having the attendees talk about people in their lives who are high-maintenance individuals. Team members who seem to fit into this category might actually be frustrated people who seek better leadership. Often companies move people into leadership simply because they're good at their jobs or as a rite of passage tied to tenure or family status. At the workshop, we asked how many attendees who were perceived as leaders had received any leadership training, and only a couple raised a hand. Why do companies persist in putting people in leadership positions without adequate preparation? To address this problem—to get the people on the bus moving in the right direction—we examined what we call The Three Significant Circles of Leadership.

Circle 1: Employ. Use the job interview to determine whether a candidate is a good fit for your company and its culture. A person who's a bad fit easily can become high maintenance in your ranks. During interviews don't only ask traditional questions like: "What are your strengths and weaknesses?" Use open-ended questions that can reveal the person's behavior patterns. For instance, ask the candidate to provide an example of how he or she resolved a work conflict with a colleague. Use phrases like "Tell me about," "Describe," and "Share with me..." Those types of questions give the candidate encouragement to share information giving you valuable insight into his or her personality. As an interviewer, try to listen more and speak less.

Circle 2: Educate. Ineffective leaders often give direction in a way that best matches their learning style, but not all learning styles are the same. The three primary learning styles are: visual - a person sees that a fire is hot and stays away, auditory - a person hears from another that a fire is hot and avoids it, and kinesthetic - a person must experience a fire to understand it is hot, so he attempts to grab the flame.

In the workshop, we facilitated an exercise to illustrate the importance of good communication. After handing everyone a piece of paper with a grid on both sides, we asked everyone to draw a profile of a pig, centered on the page, head facing left, with a portion of the pig in all grid boxes except one. We gave them one minute to complete the task. When time was up, the attendees held up their drawings. Every pig was different: some were incomplete, others were the person's own version without following directions, and some were blank pieces of paper, and so on. Next, we gave attendees written instructions on how to draw a pig and another minute to complete the task. Again, attendees produced a variety of pig drawings. Finally, we walked attendees through the process, providing a picture of a pig and an example of how to draw it. This exercise showed attendees the importance of effective communication. If you don't provide clear direction in a way your team understands, you'll never get that bus moving in the right direction.

Circle 3: Engage/Communicate. Communication is just as much what you do say as what you don't say. It's essential to praise teams when they're doing a great job. Words are only part of the person-to-person communication picture, with body language and tone playing important roles in the communication process as well.

To better communicate with our teams, it is helpful to understand individual personality styles including your own. In our workshop we use a system that categorizes people in 4 roles: the relator, the socializer, the analyzer, and the driver. A difference in personality styles can lead to communication miscues. Some examples include: assuming teams understand when they do not, providing vague instructions, not offering assistance throughout the project, and sometimes becoming exasperated and doing their tasks for them.

For example, an analyzer who most likely could create spreadsheets in her sleep asks a team member who has little experience with Excel to create a simple spreadsheet for a meeting. She provides instructions on how to enter the data and create simple graphs. A week later the analyzer asks for the spreadsheet, but it's unfinished and incorrect. The analyzer is upset, but shouldn't be. She did not provide her team member with additional guidance or direction, show them the goal or end result of what she expected, or provide a deadline. As leaders, we must clearly express our expectations and give our teams the tools to complete their assigned tasks. It's helpful to start with the outcome in mind.

Last but not least, the most important component of communication is listening, and it's a skill all good leaders want to develop and/or improve. Without good listening skills, you can't be good at interviewing, training or communicating. That's why my training includes improv exercises focused on listening.

Our workshop attracted a standing-room-only crowd, which suggests to me that attendees at the conference desire to be better leaders. You don't have to wait for a conference workshop to improve. You can sign up for third-party training programs, research leadership articles on the internet, or read books on the topic. Understanding these three circles of leadership will put you on the path to better communication skills and become the best leader you can be.

Chapter Takeaway:

_____

_____

_____

CHAPTER 42 | BATTLING WORKPLACE SABOTEURS

When a therapist really helps

Though you mostly hear about sabotage as a strategy during wartime, companies also use sabotage against their competitors, and some individuals use sabotage to advance or protect themselves at others' expense. I know all about such individuals from hard-earned personal experience and repeated tales of woe describing how someone deliberately undermined their progress. I'm here to offer suggestions and perhaps some sanity to those who find themselves in such a situation.

Saboteurs 101

Saboteurs aren't easy to recognize, which is one reason they're so insidious. They smile to your face and say what you want to hear, then say exactly the opposite to other folks when you walk away. When confronted, they deny their duplicity. Saboteurs work hard to hide their identity and eliminate any clues that could link them to their clandestine actions.

Because saboteurs are so adept at subterfuge, there are few warning signs when you meet or interview them. They often come across as charming and downright appealing. They paint a rosy picture of how they promote a team environment. They pledge support to your business initiatives. After about six months you begin to feel abandoned. The promised support is nowhere to be found. They hoard information, giving you only enough to function, which makes it difficult to succeed. If you ask them for more information, they are elusive and often claim they don't have the information you need. The saboteur ignores your cries for assistance, doesn't answer your emails, and occasionally makes you look foolish among your peers. This person has a list of excuses for not being available: He or she is busy with customers or other salespeople. Congratulations, you've been sabotaged.

You are being sabotaged if someone:

• Constantly puts you down with negative remarks and comments
• Takes ownership of your ideas
• Refuses to give credit where it is due
• Blames you when a project goes wrong—that is, throws you under the bus
• Shirks responsibility and accountability

- Blocks you from a promotion or position that could enhance your career
- Fills your head with negative thoughts by talking above your knowledge level or making offensive remarks like, "You'll do well because you're a woman."
- Undermines or fires a smart and capable team member to protect their own position
- Spends valuable work time creating drama by spreading lies and half-truths that destroy reputations and relationships. They close their office door for these conversations to add to the drama.

A colleague sabotaged me in one of my previous sales positions. He knew I could do his job and even told me so in a complimentary way; in fact, he acted as if he were mentoring me for that role. Time after time, however, he blindsided me by giving me projects that were next to impossible to accomplish. I surprised him by accomplishing these tasks. Then the personal assaults began. He told me I needed more knowledge in certain areas. He gave me "fluff" projects and asked me to do housekeeping tasks my male colleagues would never be asked to do. I gradually began to second-guess myself. Does that sound familiar? I finally left that position and rebuilt my confidence by succeeding at another sales job.

As a footnote to that story, when a neophyte in the scrap metal industry, my previous boss expressed doubts about my ability to obtain a certain account. His remark brought my experience with the saboteur back and triggered that horrible feeling. The good news is I secured the account in question and was rewarded with a bottle of Dom Perignon and a note from my boss apologizing for doubting me and promising not to do it again. And true to his word, he didn't.

Fighting Back

Do you suspect there's a saboteur in your midst? Defend yourself by following these suggestions.

Let them know you're on to them. Ask them directly, preferably with someone else in the room, about a particular remark or behavior that undermined your reputation or impeded your performance. Ask them to explain why and/or how they came to a specific conclusion about your work.

Be your own information source. If your supervisor or co-workers aren't providing the knowledge you need to succeed and advance in your job, gather it yourself through the internet, books and other sources. If possible, find someone else in the company or industry who will serve as a mentor.

Stand up for what's right. Saboteurs' deliberate obstruction, disruption or destruction in the workplace affects everyone in the company, not just those they target. The time and effort they spend weakening others to make themselves appear stronger can stop all forward motion. Start to identify ways the saboteur's actions are affecting the company as a whole. You can bring this information to the attention of a company executive, but make sure you have strong evidence to justify your position, or another job, before doing so. Saboteurs are adept at making others look and act crazy.

Know you aren't alone. Chances are someone else in the company is receiving similar treatment. If you work for a larger company, you can raise the issue with the human resources director. In smaller firms, finding another position within the company or leaving the company altogether might be your only options.

Saboteurs are an unpleasant workplace reality that can affect your job performance and overall happiness in your position. If you love your job and company, don't let a saboteur throw you off course. Let your performance speak for itself. Trust me, you can beat saboteurs by not lowering yourself to their level. But realize it's not easy.

Chapter Takeaway:

CHAPTER 43 | ON THE ROAD AGAIN

Business travel with a plan

A blessedly smooth, week-long business trip recently had me thinking about the other side of the coin: the on-the-road challenges business people face when they travel regularly. I'm not talking about travel to a luxury hotel with 900-thread-count linens, room service, and a terrycloth robe in the closet. Nor am I talking about a long day on the road in which you start from home and end at home. I mean travel that takes you to a remote, rural setting where the one motel has rooms fragrant with carpet cleaner (or, worse, insect spray) and small, stained towels—the kind of place where the person who cleans the rooms is the same one who checks you in and answers the phone.

There are centuries' worth of stories from traveling business people. If you're in sales for any length of time, you're bound to have a tale or two. Although the stories are amusing, the life of a traveling salesperson is far from glamorous. Granted, the cars, trains and airplanes we use today are faster and much more comfortable than the horse-drawn buggies that transported our forefathers but the days are long and exhausting regardless.

Don't believe me? Here's my schedule from a recent three-day road trip:

Monday: Wake at 4 a.m. to catch a 7:30 flight. After landing, head straight to a meeting and lunch with a prospect. After lunch, visit another customer en route to the hotel. Check into the hotel and then have dinner with two customers who know each other. My head hits the pillow at 11 p.m., but I don't fall asleep until about 1 a.m.

Tuesday: My alarm goes off at 6 a.m. I head to a breakfast meeting and plant tour with a customer at 7:30. Drive 3.5 hours to meet with another prospect. Meet a customer for dinner. Go to bed at 10:30 p.m. and fall asleep when my head hits the pillow.

Wednesday: Wake at 6 a.m., have breakfast, and hit the road by 7:30 for a meeting at 9:30. Drive about 30 minutes to a second meeting at 11:30. Head to the airport by 2 p.m., return the rental car, and catch my flight at 3:30.

Like many salespeople, I'm in perpetual motion when I travel, trying to optimize my time and maximize my interactions, but with little rest. Traveling to a different time zone, even just one hour away, can throw off your internal clock, making it difficult to sleep. And as anyone who travels knows, it's also difficult to sleep soundly in a hotel, especially the first night. Often there are slamming doors, refrigerators, air conditioners, other appliances, or other guests making noise. A fellow traveler gave me a tip on how to minimize such distractions: Simply unplug the noisy appliances.

I also request a room away from the elevator or the dreaded ice machine, but not too far down the hall. As a woman traveling alone, I've found it can be creepy going to a hotel room at the end of a long hallway, especially at night. I've become extremely adept at opening and shutting the door and fastening the security latch in one swift movement. I've run into some scary dudes in hotel hallways.

Maximizing the Miles

Business people must be extremely organized to remain productive while traveling and maximize the return for time invested. Making the most of your time on one trip can save you from having to repeat it later.

To minimize time in transit, know the territory you're visiting and plan your route. Various websites and smartphone applications allow you to enter starting and destination points as well as any stops in between, and they chart the most efficient route. Similarly, GPS is a must. Whether it's a built-in feature in your car or an app on your phone, this feature will save you time and frustration. GPS technology isn't 100-percent accurate, however. I can't tell you how many times my GPS has guided me to an open field in the middle of Ohio, but more often than not it will keep you on course or help you get back on track.

Speaking of technology, if you have a wireless connection in your car, travel time is ideal for catching up with customers, family, and friends— but only if you can do so safely with a hands-free device.

If I'm meeting several prospects or customers on a given day, I try to plan at least two of the get-togethers around meals. In my experience, people are more apt to make time for a meeting when a meal is involved. Such meetings are a wise use of your time, you both have to eat and a restaurant can encourage a more relaxed interaction than an office setting. Thanks to the internet, it's easy to research restaurant options before your meeting. I try to stay away from franchise eateries in favor of something a bit more original, where I can find healthier food. I once found a deli where I could gamble and purchase any needed liquor, tobacco and firearms. Surprisingly, the food was great but I opted not to do any further shopping. Everything anyone could need all in one place. Again, in Ohio.

Managing your time is always a challenge when traveling. If you get delayed at one meeting or an appointment runs late, it can mess up a whole day of meetings if you've scheduled yourself too tightly. I usually give a range of time at which I'll arrive at stops after the first appointment, then I call my contacts to let them know I'm on my way. There's nothing worse than throwing off your customer's or prospect's day because you're running behind or, in some cases, you're lost. That's why it's prudent to allow extra time in transit and ask your contacts if there are any special directions to reach their facility.

As for which transportation mode is better, that is a personal preference. Some people prefer to drive within a certain radius because it takes the same amount of time when you consider getting to the airport, going through security, and waiting to board. Driving also allows you to make several stops along the way rather than simply flying from Point A to Point B. I prefer to fly because I can answer emails and write presentations, meet potential customers on airplanes and write proposals, correspondence, and columns while waiting at the airport and sitting on the plane.

If you are a woman traveling alone, be aware and prepared. Make sure your vehicle is in good working order and you have emergency equipment like jumper cables in the trunk. Request a room closer to the front desk if the hotel is missing some light bulbs and ceiling tiles, use all the locks and don't put a room service order for breakfast on your door for the morning. It tells strangers how many people are in your room. If you find a moment to work out, get the lay of the land first. One night while running on a treadmill, I spotted a guy standing outside peering in. Disturbing beyond belief. Guess where?

Being away from your familiar environment and daily routine is the most difficult part of travel. Business travelers are human. We miss our families, our kids' baseball games, the dog and our own beds and pillows—unless, of course, we stay at a hotel with 900-thread-count linens, room service, and a terrycloth robe in the closet.

Chapter Takeaway:

CHAPTER 44 | THREE TRAITS OF EXCEPTIONAL SALESPEOPLE

Finding your own exceptional trait

I met recently with a customer on Chicago's far north side. I was there to do a KIT—keeping-in-touch—call. I intended to keep the meeting brief, a half-hour or less, so I wouldn't have to drive home to the southwest side of Chicago in Friday rush-hour traffic. You can probably guess what happened. During our conversation, my customer closed his office door and began to open up, essentially telling me his life story. In the middle of this personal conversation, he said, "I don't know why I'm telling you all of this. I think I just trust you." Even though I faced a now much longer rush-hour drive home, I stayed. Why? Because when a customer says he (or she) trusts you, you don't reply, "Nice—gotta go!" My customer's remark reminded me how trustworthiness is an attribute of exceptional business people, along with empathy and a positive attitude. Every person has unique positive traits. Here's my take of the traits I have used to build relationships that last a lifetime.

Being Trustworthy

Being worthy of someone's trust is about the highest compliment you can receive from another human being. When a business person is trustworthy, there's no limit to what he or she can accomplish. Trustworthy people can build an entire book of business on referrals. Customers, friends and acquaintances pass your name on to others based on their confidence in you. Being trustworthy, however, entails more than just being intuitive and reliable in business; the behavior must fan out to friends and family too. Otherwise, you're merely an actor. Regrettably, trustworthiness can't be taught, it's a trait each individual has to establish and earn. I know this from my years as a consultant. I help salespeople get organized, assist them in setting goals, walk them through the sales process, and help them build strong relationships—but I can't make them trustworthy. It's a character trait that comes from within.

If you want a lesson in trustworthiness, ponder what most people think about automobile salespeople. Outside of work, they might be great folks, but virtually no customer trusts them in their job. Last summer I went car shopping for my son and told the salesman the ideal vehicle would have all-wheel drive. The salesman told me his own vehicle is front-wheel drive and it works well for him in winter weather. In short, he was selling me what he wanted to sell me, not what

I wanted to buy. If he were trustworthy, he would have been more focused on fulfilling my request. He simply wanted to sell a car and not necessarily the car I wanted to buy. I ended up buying a car with front-wheel drive from that dealer because there was limited availability of vehicles with all-wheel drive in our area. A few months later, we Chicagoans faced the third-worst winter in the city's history. I'm sure my son would have found an all-wheel drive vehicle more practical, not to mention the worry element as a parent. I don't remember the salesman's name, but you can bet he won't receive a referral from me and I won't go back to that dealer either.

The Empathy Factor

In addition to trustworthiness, great business people tend to have a high capacity for empathy, which some call "life's connective tissue." Business people who are empathetic have the ability to experience the feelings, thoughts and attitudes of others around them. And it's common for them to become the confidant to many. That's part of the reason I stayed and listened to my customer in that recent meeting. If I'd stuck with my original plan and left within a half hour to avoid the rush-hour commute, I would have missed one of the finest conversations with a customer in my 30-year career. Being able to put yourself into someone else's shoes builds relationships that last a lifetime.

When a person is sensitive to the tone of a phone conversation or email, the customer appreciates that consideration. Here's one example: I was scheduled to do sales training for a company and found out days before the session that the company was planning some layoffs that would affect some of the people scheduled for my training program. I asked the sales manager if he would prefer to reschedule the training for a more opportune time. I could feel his relief and appreciation through the phone. Me, not so much, as I invested time in creating the program.

Another example of empathy comes in the sales arena when customers or prospects are too busy to take the salesperson's call. Empathetic salespeople don't assume the customer or prospect is dodging their call. They understand people are busy and don't take the delay personally. It is narcissistic of salespeople to think a refused or unanswered call is all about them.

Positive Power

A positive attitude is the third leg of the sales-success tripod. One of my mentors reminded me repeatedly, "People like to do business with people they like." Who wouldn't want to do business with someone having a positive attitude? Think about how this applies in your personal life as well. Is there one person you call when something goes right in your life? If so, chances are it's because that person has a positive attitude and will rejoice in your good fortune, not bring you down.

In addition to being a great benefit professionally, a positive attitude can bring numerous personal benefits for salespeople. Studies show, for instance, that people with a positive attitude can live longer and experience lower rates of depression, lower levels of stress, greater resistance to colds, better overall well-being, and reduced risk of death from cardiovascular disease. Positive people also display better coping skills during times of hardship and stress—helpful abilities for any professional.

I'm glad I took the time to listen to my customer's life story that day, and I hope he entrusted me with that personal information because he saw in me the three traits I've addressed here. If I'd followed my own agenda, our relationship would have remained status quo rather than status "grow", which would have been a loss for both of us. As I learned about his life, I experienced the value of empathy, trust and positive attitude in every relationship.

Chapter Takeaway:

CHAPTER 45 | CREATING A SALES GAME PLAN

Why a vision helps to guide the team

The start of a new year is exciting, in part because it's the season of football playoffs and in part because it's an opportunity to set new goals. Instead of focusing only on individual goals, as I've done in previous chapters, I'll turn the spotlight on company goals. It is important for your company to create a game plan and share that vision.

Your sales team is eager to begin its year poised for sales success. Not having a company sales plan is like putting the team on the field without a strategy. You might score occasionally, but it's more likely to be chaos. Without guidance, the players are going to focus on their own performance more than the overall team effort and the team is going to lose.

In sports, the ultimate goal for any team is winning a championship. Being from Chicago, I've cheered for numerous teams in the chase for a championship, including the Bulls, Bears, White Sox and Blackhawks and Cubs. What those winning teams had in common when they won a championship are excellent leadership and clearly defined goals. In your company, what will make your sales group a championship team? Who's responsible for developing and rolling out a game plan to engage them? Where can your salespeople go for coaching and training? Championship sales teams don't win by chance. They ask the tough questions and put in the hard work.

Setting the goal

You can base goals for your company and sales department on revenue, profit, new business, growth, volume, team performance or any combination of those measures. There are pros and cons to all of the above. Take into account the strengths of your team when deciding which goals are achievable.

Sales revenue. Using sales revenue alone as your main goal can be tricky. If you set revenue goals too low, your team may achieve them quickly and easily. In some cases, when leadership sees the sales team fast approaching the goal line, they extend the line further. Such an act comes across as the worst kind of bait-and-switch and will alienate the sales team, especially if the goals are tied to compensation.

It's similarly unwise to set the goal so high that it's unachievable. When making sales revenue your goal, I recommend offering an incremental reward such as increasing the commission or bonus from 10 to 15 percent. As a salesperson or the team reaches the stated revenue mark they receive that incremental benefit in their paycheck. That keeps everyone motivated and gives them an immediate reward for their efforts rather than making them wait to reach a single, long-term goal.

Profit. I've always found profit-based commissions or bonuses attractive. Even when I was bartending for extra income in my 20s, I asked the bar owner for a percentage of the evening's till rather than taking tips. The owner loved my approach and I always made more than the tip-chasers, also, I didn't have to be nice to customers I didn't like! Basing sales rewards on profits also teaches salespeople how to set prices and understand operating expenses. It's a win-win when structured properly. To summarize, if your profitability metrics are confusing or if you change them arbitrarily to decrease the sales team's reward, then your incentive system will fail. Good salespeople can survive in such an environment, but you won't earn their loyalty. Eventually they'll move to another company with more supportive, less manipulative business practices.

New business. Making the acquisition of new business your principal sales target is a wonderful way to grow a company and replace whatever customers you lose through attrition. Make sure, however, that the focus on new business generation doesn't allow your salespeople to become obsessed with finding new customers at the expense of serving existing ones. Instead, try combining new business acquisition with customer retention goals and cumulative objectives for the entire sales team. The team will work together to achieve the objectives, cheering each other on and clearing the way into the end zone.

Company growth. If you make company growth the goal for your sales team, make sure the targets are challenging yet achievable. For example, if you want to increase your company's gross annual sales from $10 million to $20 million in five years, map out a strategy for achieving that level on a realistic, attainable timeline. Consider the types of companies to target as well as logistics, operating expenses, and profit margins—and, as always, don't focus on new growth at the expense of current customers. When your company reaches its growth target, be sure there's a reward. If the team plays and wins the Super Bowl of Sales and there's no personal gain at the end, your best players will become free agents.

The Benefits of Teamwork

Setting a team sales goal is an approach I recommend for companies with an exceptional coach at the helm. Smart play calling, adequate protection from the front line, and a gutsy catch will lead the squad to victory. If only one person shows up ready to play, there is no team effort and defeat is certain. Although I believe individual goals are important, I like having them tied to team goals. Rewarding your salespeople for teamwork will create a positive culture, encourage mentoring, create leaders, and keep everyone focused.

My point is simply this: Play to win. Don't wait for more than 100 years to win a championship (sorry Cubs fans!). Develop a sales game plan and get your team into the game. With the right approach and guidance, the team members will begin to perform like the champions you expect.

Chapter Takeaway:

CHAPTER 46 | OUT WITH THE OLD, IN WITH THE NEW

How changing behaviors can create a better culture

In 1967, scientist G.R. Stephenson conducted an experiment in which he used blasts of air to train adult rhesus monkeys to avoid manipulating an object. He then placed an untrained monkey in a cage along with the trained one and the object in question, giving the untrained monkey the opportunity to watch the trained one behave fearfully in the object's presence. When they were later tested separately, three of the four untrained monkeys showed fear of the object, which suggests they had learned that fear from observing the behavior of their trained counterparts.

Like those monkeys, humans pick up cues from the actions of those around them, for better and for worse. You can see this phenomenon play out in the workplace when a new employee challenges the status quo. Fear and other emotions prompt the majority to nip such efforts in the bud. Why? Because they don't want to face change, because everything is OK just the way it is. It's the "that's how it's done around here" mentality.

I see this all too frequently when I'm training salespeople having various levels of experience. In every group there is at least one person with crossed arms, waiting to attack the first co-worker who even thinks about embracing the new knowledge.

How do you know if you and your salespeople are holding on to outdated sales ideas and practices? Tag along on a sales call and observe them in action. Here are eight old approaches with corresponding updated versions.

OLD: Quoting prices merely to entice the customer. This no longer works and hasn't for quite some time, especially if you want to achieve profitability. Today's buyers are much more informed and sophisticated—and less swayed by price alone. I shout that message from the rooftops every chance I get because it's gospel. Starting with price creates an uncomfortable relationship of distrust between the salesperson, who thinks the customer will bolt when someone else offers a better price, and the customer, who doesn't believe the salesperson's pricing is valid compared with their competition. As one publication noted recently, "a customer who makes a decision on price alone is only a rented customer."

NEW: Quoting realistic pricing to create realistic relationships.

OLD: Asking a prospect a barrage of questions seeking basic facts, such as "What are your volumes?", "How often does that happen?", and "Who is your current vendor?" To the prospect, that approach is like facing a firing squad and the relationship starts out with a negative connotation.

NEW: Developing open-ended questions that allow your prospect to talk. It's an unselfish type of sales call. Try it.

OLD: Thinking you're more knowledgeable than the potential customer. Most information is at everyone's fingertips through a simple search. Salespeople are no longer educating their prospects and customers but rather collaborating and finding efficiencies. If you still view yourself as the slick salesperson who's going to school or manipulate the prospect, think again. Prospects will size you up, spit you out, and find someone who knows how to be a partner in their business success.

NEW: Knowing as much as you can about a prospect's or customer's business and being prepared to contribute to its success.

OLD: Thinking all prospects are alike. For example, if you meet with someone who is a generation or two younger than you and you don't incorporate technology, you are wasting your time. No millennial wants to move backward to accommodate you. Although they aren't automatically opposed to working with someone in their parents' generation, they want client portals, pricing, and dynamic reporting and someone who understands modern business technology.

NEW: Embracing, learning and encouraging new technology in your company and sales strategies.

OLD: Talking your way through a sales call to fill the "air time." The new sales call is one of interaction, preferably with the prospect speaking 80 percent of the time and you listening 100 percent of the time. Interrupting the prospect or customer so you can speak is unacceptable.

NEW: Learn to become a better listener and practice, practice, practice.

OLD: Criticizing the competition. It might make you feel good, but it's a cardinal sin for a salesperson today. With the internet, it takes moments to find out if your critiques are true. I've said it before and I'll say it again, I learned early in life that telling on my brother when he did something bad didn't necessarily make me look good and often backfired. Remember you're not in the business of bad-mouthing anyone or anything and is unprofessional.

NEW: Refusing to get caught up in the minutiae of negativity in your business and personal life keeps you above the fray. Take the high road and develop a reputation that precedes you in the industry. A good reality check is to ask people in your company how they think your competitors would describe them. Would they say you're above the fray?

OLD: Not having a sales plan. I'm a firm believer in daily, weekly, monthly and annual goals. Planning based on goal setting is crucial in the quest for sales success and your sanity. Simply responding to situations as they develop is no longer enough.

NEW: Be the master of your sales efforts, not a victim of events as they unfold. Assert more control and direction. Decide on a sales style, approach, and desired results. Set goals and outline how and when you plan to achieve them.

OLD: Believing you have nothing left to learn. "It isn't what you don't know that gets you into trouble; it's what you know for sure that just isn't so." What do you know that might be holding you back?

BOTTOM LINE. Update your sales approach as often you change the oil in your car.

Chapter Takeaway:

CHAPTER 47 | GETTING THE BEST ROI FROM YOUR CONFERENCE INVESTMENT

Tips for before, during and after a tradeshow

When I attend any business conference or convention, my goal is always the same: To maximize the return on my investment of time, money and effort in attending. It takes a bit of planning and strategy, but it's not as difficult as you might think. Here are a few suggestions to help you get the highest value from your conference experiences.

Planting and Reaping the Rewards

After I register for an event, I set to work planning my schedule because getting the best ROI depends heavily on time management. To me, every conference is a race against time in which I always have more on my to-do list than time to do it.

Wander the web. The first task is checking the conference website often for information about who is attending and which vendors are exhibiting. From those lists, I create a "hit list" of existing contacts I need to see, prospects I want to meet, and individuals I want to see for reasons other than business, i.e., they are fun. Don't wait to do this until you arrive at the conference. That's like not opening a textbook until the night before the exam—you know who you are. If that's how you approach events, your chances for a strong ROI are greatly diminished.

Scope out the schedule. Take time to study the conference schedule and high-light the networking events (including lunches and dinners) and workshops you'd like to attend. Prioritize essential programs over second-choice sessions. I enter those details into my Outlook calendar. Add the conference event schedule to your Outlook calendar. One time, I sent a meeting invitation to a contact with the location marked as "Pool"—otherwise, the meeting probably wouldn't have happened! By the time I arrive at the conference, my calendar is full and the details are in my smartphone, easily accessible and ready to remind me of my next appointment. Occasionally, I'm invited to events after I arrive at a conference, so I try to leave some flexibility in my schedule.

Peruse the property. After getting settled at a conference, I like taking a walk to get the lay of the land and scout out quiet places where I can meet with customers and prospects. One of my colleagues made it his modus operandi to reserve a poolside cabana that was fully stocked with food and drink where he would host back-to-back appointments all day long. Although the non-stop networking was exhausting for him, it was relaxing and memorable for his clients (and for me, as I was invited to enjoy the hospitality).

Partake of the programming. When it comes to conference workshops, the list of reasons for attending is as long as my arm. Education is a principal reason, but there are other, more strategic reasons as well. You can gain intelligence on competitors who are exhibiting or serving on panel discussions, network with those on your hit list who attend the same workshop, or show up just to be seen there. For example, if you are interested in working with a company that will absolutely attend a certain workshop and you don't, it is a mistake for a couple of reasons: One, you're assuming you have nothing to learn; two, you're assuming there's no one beneficial to meet there. You're most likely wrong on both counts.

Explore the expo. If the conference has an exhibition, be sure to walk the floor. I know folks who brag they never set foot in exhibit halls. I can only imagine the opportunities they have lost. I try to walk through the hall more than once to make sure I capitalize on all networking or information-gathering opportunities. The last day or final hours of trade shows often are ideal to claim uninterrupted time with potential vendors and customers. Don't forget that exhibitors' ROI depends on attendees walking the floor; you are helping them when you create some traffic at their booths.

Maintain order. During the conference, it's important to stay organized. Write reminder notes on collected business cards; keep receipts in one place for your expense report; write summaries of workshops you've attended; and outline action items for later. Your smartphone or tablet can help with all of those tasks. Download apps to help you organize the business cards and receipts. You might view those steps as excessive, but I say they're necessary. Otherwise, you spend your first day back from the conference on a treasure hunt trying to decipher why you have some stranger's business card, why you can't remember those helpful facts from that interesting workshop, and locating the $58 parking receipt for reimbursement.

Talk the talk. My favorite part of any conference is the networking, also called schmoozing. Most conference attendees enjoy meeting their customers, new acquaintances/prospects and friends at a common gathering place at the event hotel. Although such interactions don't sound like downtime, they are—at least by conference standards. While schmoozing isn't for everyone, it's a skill you might want to develop to benefit both you and your company. If you truly aren't the networking type, shadow a friend who has that skill and you might soon find yourself learning the art. Think of it like playing ping-pong—once you try a few volleys, it's easy and even fun.

When the conference is over and you head back to your office, immediately cultivate what you've sown. Poor follow-up is why nearly 80 percent of all connections made at conferences don't become customers. Conferences are expensive in every aspect; time, dollars and loss of sleep. Make sure you get the ROI you deserve before you leave and hit the ground running when you return.

Chapter Takeaway:

_____

_____

_____

CHAPTER 48 | DEVELOPING A SALES AND MARKETING PLAN

Creating, executing and leading

Do you remember the first lemonade stand you had as a kid? I certainly remember mine. I lived on a busy street with people walking by all day long, so I already had the most important element—a good location. My marketing process began by gathering art supplies, finding a cardboard box, and constructing a sign that advertised the product (lemonade) and price (10 cents a glass). For effect, I drew a picture of a person smiling as he consumed his refreshing glass of lemonade. I then pillaged the lemonade ingredients and glasses from my parents' pantry, which lowered my overhead. The next step was to set up a presentable sales table with two chairs: one for the cashier (my friend Linda), the other for the salesperson (me). It was my job to make sure people didn't walk by without at least thinking about buying our thirst-quenching product. Even as 6-year-olds, we knew the importance of sales and marketing.

Unfortunately, I find time and time again that companies don't give their sales process the same attention as other aspects of their business. Salespeople are the face of your company and the reason why customers decide to sign a contract, remain your customer, or return after leaving. Planning to invest in hard assets like property, buildings, and equipment doesn't make sense when you haven't planned how you'll bring in the business needed to justify and pay for the other parts.

Coming Up With a Plan

The sales and marketing teams in your company will work best when given a plan and a budget. Those elements are also important to investors or financiers who will want to know how you intend to reach your target market and gain market share. A well-written sales plan includes forecasting. Fortunately, you don't need a degree in business, mathematics or economics to do it. The process is nothing more than educated guessing. When I began my scrap metal business I knew how many companies we needed to service per day to cover our overhead and have a little extra for unforeseen circumstances. My approach wasn't sophisticated—and I had only a calculator to help me—but it worked. Today, computers and small-business management and budgeting software make the task much easier.

Before you develop a sales plan, you need to candidly assess who is at the helm of your sales team. Does the person have the skills to develop such a plan and the dedication to implement it? At many companies, the answer is an emphatic "no". If your company lacks someone internally who can get the job done, consider hiring a consultant.

The first step toward developing a basic sales plan is having the leadership team establish sales goals and objectives. My sales mentor used to say, "If you don't know where you're going, any road will take you there." To put it another way, if you don't have a target, how can you ever hope to hit anything? Begin by assessing your company's current market share and then developing one-, three-, and five-year sales goals and objectives. What is your company's size now, and how large do you want to become? Do you aspire to be regional, national or global? Map out the reach. Which customers will you target to get there? What are your biggest revenue drivers? What are the logistics you'll need to serve those customers? What are your company's strengths and weaknesses? Who are your company's main competitors and what strategies are in place against them? This kind of corporate soul-searching will allow you to develop realistic goals.

Once you identify your targeted customer base, develop a pricing strategy—preferably one that accounts for operating costs and debt. Then determine who calls on which prospect or customer. Nothing looks worse to a prospect than sales team members who are unaware of what their colleagues are doing. Not only does it look like there's no communication in the company, it also wastes money for multiple people to call on the same company, especially if no one lands the account. There are lots of wheels running without forward motion. Certainly not a recipe for success.

There should be a clear understanding of the plan's overall goals in terms of winning new business, growing the current book of business, and increasing profitability. The plan's ultimate purpose is to outline the revenue generation structure for your company. It should include periodic (daily, weekly, monthly, quarterly) productivity goals for your salespeople. These markers will help them understand how their efforts support the company in meeting production goals. Be certain each goal has a deadline and is measurable. And it's nice to reward your salespeople when they reach these goals.

Marketing is an important part of your sales plan. This is a good time to reassess your company's website, social media presence, printed collateral, exhibition plans, advertising and promotional items. If these materials don't carry a consistent message, appearance, and complement each other; they'll be confusing and give people the impression your company isn't well organized and professional. For example, I recently visited a website where the verbiage wasn't consistent, stating that the company serves 800 customers on one page, 1,200 on another page, and 900 on yet another page. It was an embarrassment.

Making the Plan Work

As much as possible, stick to the direction you choose in your sales and marketing plan. If you allow too much wiggle room, it's easy to veer off course. At the same time, it's important to review the plan and progress at least quarterly. During the review, it's OK to make adjustments. After all, markets and technology change so quickly it's inevitable you'll have to make some tweaks. Of course your options will depend on which direction your company defined at the start.

As each year winds down, make the sales and marketing plan one of your goals for the next year. It will help your sales team stay focused and your bottom line will benefit from your efforts—just as mine did at the lemonade stand.

Chapter Takeaway:

CHAPTER 49 | THE LEARNING IMPERATIVE

Luxury or necessity

At a recent industry networking event, I talked with several veterans who had attended my sales sessions in years past. Some thanked me for the sales tips and recited their learning experience as if they were there yesterday, others reminisced about the improv games experience or the T-shirt giveaways. It was gratifying to hear I was able to help in their careers and provide them a cool shirt to wear when hitting the gym or mowing the lawn. Their enthusiasm prompted me to ask what other training they'd had since my sessions. Their answer? None.

Why don't companies offer training to their sales, marketing or customer service teams? I asked that of attendees and exhibitors at a convention. The most common reasons were cost and time, but there were others. Some respondents were fuzzy about what training entails. Others thought their company is too small for training. And still others believe hiring seasoned salespeople precludes the need for training, or think it's enough to simply pass along their own sales knowledge. Or my favorite, let them "learn the hard way," as they did.

From my informal survey, it was clear that too many companies view sales training as a luxury rather than a necessity. For progressive companies, the exact opposite is true. Training is just as essential for salespeople as it is for other business professionals. After all, at the dawn of cable, we viewed it as a luxury and now it is something most would not live without. If you need brain surgery, would you be satisfied with a first year med student, or would you want the most highly trained brain surgeon you could find?

I also conducted an email poll of my business contacts, asking which all-important tool they use daily. Nearly everyone answered that it was their smartphone or tablet. Then I asked how they ensure the device keeps working. "By charging it regularly", they answered. Now imagine the salespeople in your company are themselves the all-important tools. They need to be charged just like the phone.

Fortunately, the electricity needed to keep a sales team fresh and aggressive comes in several forms including: team building, motivational exercises, coaching and sales training. I trained one team for over a year. The company owner was impressed with the enthusiasm, teamwork and results. He then asked me to develop a weekly coaching program to keep his team energized. He was then able to spend his time and talents better by focusing on growing the company, which he later sold for a lot of money.

Making the Training Decision

Before pursuing a sales training program, identify the goals you'd like to achieve. This will help determine the type of training your company needs and allow the trainer to customize the right program for your team.

Find a trainer who understands your business. If there's a disconnect, your salespeople will mentally check out of the training. It's equally important to find an engaging program. Because the average person can listen attentively for only about 17 minutes, interaction is a must. When choosing an instructor be sure to understand the pricing structure such as the number of participants or other additional costs.

If you decide to provide sales training, have a discussion about making it mandatory or optional. There are pros and cons to both. But be aware of those who attend and don't want to be there can be disruptive.

As stated in a previous chapter, training works best when leadership is involved—the old follow-the-leader concept. If high-level leaders show that the training is important enough to devote their time to it, then the sales team will value it even more. Leadership's involvement implies there is always room for learning. If leadership hasn't been participating in the training, it may be difficult to sustain the information presented during the training.

Sales training is an ongoing commitment; so don't expect to meet all of your training needs in one or two days. It's difficult for people to absorb masses of information in a short time; it's better to schedule the training over a few months. Schedule refresher training six months after the initial program to revisit the key points. At this time, work with the trainer to survey the participants and evaluate the results. As part of your onboarding process be sure that new hires have the same training opportunities as their teammates.

An Investment, Not a Cost

While cost is the biggest hurdle when considering sales training, consider the cost of providing nothing. Their sales success is your leadership success. It's understandable that training becomes more difficult to justify during challenging economic times. But when it comes to survival of the fittest, which companies emerge victorious? Those having the smartest and most efficient salespeople.

At another networking event, I asked a newcomer in his industry about the training in his prior sales position in finance. He replied "sure", as if it were a natural part of any career. I asked what he gained from the training and he shared sales methods and psychologies he learned that moved a prospect closer to taking action. This young man knows the value of acquiring new information to assist him in achieving his goals. If his new company stops that flow of new information, he will move on and I don't blame him.

Because I practice what I preach, in the last six months I attended a sales training webinar and an improv class. Although I've been around awhile, I continually train to keep my skills sharp and myself charged—just like my smartphone.

Chapter Takeaway:

_____

_____

_____

CHAPTER 50 | LONG-TERM SUCCESS IN SCRAP

My love letter to the recycling industry

This article was written as a love letter to the industry that embraced and affirmed me when I needed it and has sustained me from that day forward. I have no doubt there are other industries and scenarios to which this article applies. Writing a love letter to an industry for which you have passion will be twofold. It will move both you and the recipients to a grateful place. This column received phone calls and emails from all over the country When you finish reading this chapter, I ask you to write your own love letter or at least set a goal to write one.

Dear Recyclers,

Do you remember the day you entered the recycling industry? Maybe you wanted a job, any job, and thought it would be a stepping stone to something else. Perhaps you viewed it as a wise career move. Then again, maybe you were the fourth generation to enter your family's business. Regardless, I firmly believe that once you enter this industry, it's difficult to leave. I have a few theories about why that is the case.

You make a difference. When you work in recycling, you're helping to recover and reuse valuable raw materials, which saves energy, preserves natural resources, and protects the environment. What you do is important and interesting (which comes in handy at cocktail parties). In short, you're doing the right thing for the planet and making a difference in a tangible way. Who'd want to give up that sense of gratification?

Every day is different. No two days in the recycling business are alike, which means it's never boring. It's like working in an emergency room, you never know what is going to happen. Markets change by the minute. Companies start up, merge and go bankrupt with amazing speed. There are daily challenges with safety, sales and marketing, logistics, and processing equipment. The pace is quick; the competition is fierce; and the compliance requirements are never-ending. Most recycling professionals end their days not knowing where the time went—a sure sign that your occupation is fast-paced and engaging.

The people are great and the stories are plentiful. No industry has a more multitalented and amazing cast of characters than the recycling industry, which welcomes people from all walks of life, experience and age levels and from all over the world. It seems to attract and create interesting people with each having intriguing tales to tell. If you work in the business long enough, you'll be one of them. In my recycling career, I've learned from some of the best industry veterans, watched family-oriented businesses grow and prosper, been a player in the corporate scrap world, and been humbled by recyclers' immense generosity—and I've met many memorable people all along the way.

Experience is valued. Recycling is definitely an industry in which experience matters. Recycling companies mix older teams with less-experienced workers, creating strong mentorship opportunities and cross-generational cultures. Unlike other business sectors that push veterans out the door, the recycling industry veterans often work well into their 60s, 70s, 80s and even 90s. Though markets, materials, regulations and processes change, experienced recycling professionals bring immutable value to the table and a comforting calm during drastic market fluctuations. I once provided sales training for a company with a salesman in his 80s. He didn't stick around for much of the training, but he showed up every day for the free lunch, and each of us at the table collected valuable nuggets just from being in his presence.

There's room to grow. The ever-changing nature of the recycling industry offers an opportunity to learn something new every day. The industry sees constant flux in recycling processes and technologies, sales and marketing approaches, safety and environmental regulations, competition, and material types, among other areas.

Job or Career?

For a long and successful career, it's key to grow and change professionally along with the industry. This means being in an environment where this is possible. Though good leaders in any company will encourage talented team members to take on greater challenges, larger companies more routinely move them up through the ranks. Smaller companies are more likely to keep people in silos until a leadership position opens up—which might not be until an existing leader retires or expires. If you hope to move into leadership, ask about your employer's approach to career development. Waiting for someone to expire is not a good strategy.

Choose the right company and leader for yourself. With a company that doesn't meet your values or having an ineffective leader, you cannot reach your full potential. Have regular discussions with leadership about your future, no matter where you work.

To improve your chances of success, here are **6 things not to do:**

1. **Don't jump around from company to company.** Don't fall into thinking the opportunities will be better elsewhere, they usually aren't.

2. **Don't bad-mouth your competition.** You never know when you might have to work with or for them due to a merger or buyout. Bad-mouthing other people and companies does as much damage to your reputation as it does to those you're criticizing.

3. **Don't hold grudges.** They eat away at you from the inside and they become an obsession that keeps you off balance and unable to move forward effectively. As one saying goes, "Holding a grudge is like drinking poison and waiting for the other person to die."

4. **Don't ignore or avoid your competitors.** Review their websites, read articles about them, and be sociable at industry functions. Competition is good for everyone. No one would watch professional sports if there were only one team on the field. Competition keeps us fresh, sharp and striving forward. Your only chance of keeping ahead of your competitors is to be informed about them.

5. **Don't try to be a one-person show.** Smaller companies rely on a few people to do it all. When I owned my scrap metal company, I did every job at one time or another. The constant zigzag of my days kept me from doing what I do best—sales. Hiring key people in operations allowed me to concentrate on improving sales and growing my company. I've learned it's healthy to admit there are people who can do some tasks better than I can.

6. **Don't be afraid of change.** If your company is still "old-school"— with workers filling out forms manually, using old technology and antiquated equipment—you need to change or get out. Work your way up or rust your way out or your competition is going to eat you alive.

For me and those I have met along the way, accepting a job in the recycling industry was a life-changing decision giving us an unexpected home and passion. There's a reason why we in the business say "Recycling gets in your blood." It becomes part of our professional DNA, making it impossible to be happy working anywhere else.

Thank you recycling industry for your support and encouragement. I have been fortunate to be able to help others every day of my career, all while making an impact on the environment.

Yours in Scrap,

Judy Ferraro

ACKNOWLEDGEMENTS

When my readers suggested I capture a decade of *On Sales* columns written for *Scrap Magazine* and create a book for business people, I was truly unaware of what an undertaking it would be. The first task was collecting the articles which needed updating as they contained words like "fax machine" and "Blackberry" and began rewriting to keep them current. Because I no longer like the word "management" and opt for "leadership" instead, I went through every column and made that edit. After that, I realized what looks right in a column doesn't necessarily transition fluidly to book-form. Again, more edits. Changing sentences, recalling topics previously discussed and on and on. It was never-ending. What initially seemed like a project I could easily knock out in a couple of months, turned into two years of reading, writing, rereading and re-writing!

Thank you to my friends at *Scrap Magazine*. Kent Kiser, Publisher, and Rachel Pollack, Editor in Chief, who for over a decade have edited my columns into a much better version of my initial creation. Writing the "On Sales" column has been a highlight in my life. Getting to know both of you on a personal level has been both my honor and my pleasure.

As I began the *On Sales, Leadership & Other Helpful Business Stuff* project, Christina Koenig read the manuscript making edits and brilliant suggestions on ways to turn the book into a resource guide for my readers. Thank you Christina for always being my cohort. I ask for your help because you are talented and enjoy every moment we work together. Plus the fun-factor is always in play.

As in my previous book, Marie Carberry, created another terrific book cover and took over the formatting responsibilities. I cannot thank you enough for your patience as this project was in the works for over two years.

Thank you Lisa Heniff for coordinating my beautification for the book cover photo. The early morning transformation turned out well, perhaps a miracle, in lieu of the restless night before.

When writing a book, there comes a time when you can no longer identify the errors in your work. Thank you to Mary Wood, a college speech instructor and English teacher and Ruth Ferraro, a business professional and my sister-in-law, who took the time to assist in the editing process. It is exhausting work. I am grateful for your expertise and your friendships.

Like a knight in shining armor, my good friend Lamb Chop (a.k.a. LC, Tom Sammon) jumped into action when I needed him. There were hours of reading, writing, editing, rereading and re-editing. It was fun to collaborate with him and I have a feeling this will not be our only venture. Tom, your business prowess, sense of humor and excellent writing skills are evident in every chapter. Thank you for all you have done to assist me in completing this project and for all the writing tips I acquired along the way.

When writing a book, the author gets to a point where the errors are invisible to their eye. Enter my girlfriends and word hawks, Mary Ann Bachelor, Joan Howard, Therese Thompson, Sharilyn Van Wyhe and Gloria Virtel. Thank you for your keen eye and attention to detail. I appreciate your time, comments, suggestions and most of all, your friendships.

And last but not least to my gentle husband Michael Gruber and loving son Eric who are and will always be the loves of my life.

Notes:

36111737R00091

Made in the USA
Middletown, DE
25 October 2016